WEYERHAEUSER ENVIRONMENTAL BOOKS

William Cronon, Editor

Weyerhaeuser Environmental Books explore human relationships with natural environments in all their variety and complexity. They seek to cast new light on the ways that natural systems affect human communities, the ways that people affect the environments of which they are a part, and the ways that different cultural conceptions of nature profoundly shape our sense of the world around us. A complete list of the books in the series appears at the end of this book.

T0339255

Nature
Next Door

Cities and Trees in the American Northeast

ELLEN STROUD

Foreword by William Cronon

UNIVERSITY OF WASHINGTON PRESS   SEATTLE & LONDON

Nature Next Door is published with the assistance of a grant from the Weyerhaeuser Environmental Books Endowment, established by the Weyerhaeuser Company Foundation, members of the Weyerhaeuser family, and Janet and Jack Creighton.

© 2012 by the University of Washington Press
First paperback edition © 2013 by the University of Washington Press
Printed and bound in the United States of America
18 17 16 15 14   5 4 3 2

University of Washington Press
PO BOX 50096, Seattle, WA 98145, USA
www.washington.edu/uwpress

Library of Congress Cataloging-in-Publication Data
Stroud, Ellen. Nature next door : cities and trees in the American Northeast /
Ellen Stroud ; foreword by William Cronon.
p. cm. — (Weyerhaeuser environmental books)
Includes bibliographical references and index.
ISBN 978-0-295-99331-7 (pbk. : alk. paper)
1. Trees in cities—Northeastern States. 2. Urban forestry—Northeastern States.
3. Urban ecology (Sociology)—Northeastern States. 4. Urbanization—Environmental
aspects—Northeastern States. 5. Reforestation—Northeastern States. 6. Watersheds—
Northeastern States. 7. Northeastern States—Environmental conditions. I. Title
SB435.52.N58S77 2012   582.160974—DC23   2012015579

Printed and bound in the United States of America
Designed by Ashley Saleeba
Composed in Adobe Caslon Old Style; display type set in Bauer Bodoni

The paper used in this publication is acid-free and meets the minimum requirements of American National Standard for Information Sciences— Permanence of Paper for Printed Library Materials, ANSI z39.48–1984.∞

FOR MY MOTHER, JAMIE STROUD,

AND IN MEMORY OF MY FATHER, BILL STROUD.

AND ALSO FOR THEIR GRANDCHILDREN,

NEVAEH WILLIAMS PAIGE,

CONNOR HENSON-STROUD,

AND RUBY HENSON-STROUD.

Contents

The Once and Future Forest

William Cronon

In 1983, I published a small volume entitled *Changes in the Land: Indians, Colonists, and the Ecology of New England.* That book is now nearly thirty years old, making it an early contribution to what is now regarded as the first generation of environmental history writing in the United States. In it, I told the story of how landscapes and ecosystems previously inhabited primarily by native peoples were altered by the invasion, occupation, and settlement of New England by colonists from the far side of the Atlantic. Although the resulting changes were myriad, among the most dramatic and far-reaching was deforestation. A region that had previously been well over 75 percent forested had by the middle of the nineteenth century become more than 75 percent *de*forested. In place of the woodlands that had once so astonished the colonists with their abundance, I wrote, "New England had become a world of fields and fences."

So extraordinary was this transformation that it became a source of considerable concern for New Englanders and others in the American Northeast by the time of the Civil War. In 1864, the Vermont politician and polymath George Perkins Marsh published a remarkably influential volume entitled *Man and Nature: Or, Physical Geography as Modified by Human Action* about the ways past civilizations had altered their surrounding landscapes over the long sweep of human history. His principal concern was the deforestation he had been witnessing all his life, first in northern New England and then in the Mediterranean Basin, where he served as an American diplomat starting in the 1850s. In Marsh's view, the great civilizations of antiquity—in Greece, Rome, and the Middle East—had destroyed their own prosperity by cutting trees too profligately. *Man and Nature*—which we have reprinted as a Weyerhaeuser Environmental Classic, along with with a first-rate biography of Marsh by David Lowenthal—became the founding text of the American conservation movement and is today widely regarded as one of the three most important books about the environment written by an American author, in company with Aldo Leopold's *A Sand County Almanac* and Rachel Carson's *Silent Spring*. In *Man and Nature*, the deforestation of modern New England joined that of antiquity as a symbol of environmental destruction—and as a prophetic warning that the United States might go the way of Rome if it failed to change its ways.

I share all this in part to affirm that Ellen Stroud's book *Nature Next Door: Cities and Trees in the American Northeast* explores a topic that is of much more than regional significance. The deforestation of New England, New York, and Pennsylvania did in fact help set in motion debates more than a hundred years ago that inspired the Progressive conservation movement nationwide. But partly because of those debates, the story of northeastern forests is a good deal more complicated—and much more interesting—than the simple narrative of deforestation told in my own *Changes in the Land* might lead one to believe. Anyone who visits the region today will encounter some of the most heavily forested landscapes anywhere in the United States. Indeed, such forests have become so common that when one sees a stunningly beautiful image like the one on the cover of this book, one thinks instantly of Vermont or New England or the Catskills or Adirondacks. That this image is so strongly in our minds even though the Northeast is among the most heavily urbanized areas of the United States makes these iconic wooded hillsides all the more intriguing. Rather astonishingly, a landscape that was more than three-fourths forested when the Pilgrims landed at Plymouth in 1620, and that was more than three-fourths deforested when Henry David Thoreau made his retreat to Walden in the late 1840s, is today more than three-fourths forested once again.

How trees returned to the Northeast is the puzzle Ellen Stroud pieces together so elegantly in this important new book. The traditional explanation of reforestation in the region is that market forces and interregional competition with farmers on the Midwestern prairies drove northeastern farmers out of business. Once they were no longer tending their fields, forests returned more or less on their own in response to agricultural abandonment. Although Stroud affirms that such processes certainly did occur, her great contribution is to demonstrate that this is much too simple an explanation for how the ubiquitous pastures of the nineteenth century were replaced by the equally ubiquitous forests we see today. In so doing, she offers a cautionary tale that has profound implications for environmental policy in the twenty-first century.

According to Stroud, there was nothing accidental about the way forests returned to the Northeast. In part responding to the warnings Marsh had made so persuasively in *Man in Nature*, politicians, corporations, private citizens, and governments began systematically in the second half of the nineteenth century to protect existing forests and to encourage the return of trees to lands that had lost them. Diverse topographies, economies, and political cultures meant that forest policies wound up varying dramatically from state to state. This is why Stroud chooses to organize her book in chapters that focus first on Pennsylvania, then New Hampshire, then Vermont, then Maine. (The New York story, especially in the Adirondacks, is better known, and so supplies part of the larger context that fleshes out Stroud's analysis for the region as a whole.) What she finds is that individual leadership mattered enormously, as did the mixture of industries that shaped the economy of a given state—and especially the laws governing how woodlands were taxed. Arcane as tax policy can sometimes seem, Stroud makes it far more interesting than one might imagine by helping us understand the crucial role it played in shaping the return of forests from Maine to Pennsylvania.

I will leave the particulars of this complex story to Stroud herself. *Nature Next Door* represents a remarkable feat of distillation, never oversimplifying the complex processes that brought forests back to the Northeast but also never overwhelming the reader with excessive detail. To invoke the obvious metaphor, Stroud does a masterful job of never losing sight of the forest for the trees, but she also never forgets that trees really do matter. Because there were quite different trees in Pennsylvania than there were in Maine or New Hampshire, we need to pay attention to how such differences expressed themselves in these different localities. Stroud is utterly persuasive that we need to look closely at particular places, particular ecosystems, and, just as importantly, particular institutions and policies if we are to draw the right lessons about the environmental challenges that northeastern conservationists faced in the late nineteenth and early twentieth centuries.

The northeastern forests we experience today are as much the products of human history, human culture, and human politics as they are of natural processes. Forests in the region today are utterly different from the ones over which Indians and colonists contended in the seventeenth century—and this will be as true of forests in the future as it is of those in the past. It would be foolish indeed to believe that if we simply adopted a hands-off attitude toward such matters, nonhuman nature on its own would yield the results we desire. In places like the Northeast, even wild nature is right next door, so the decisions we make about how people choose to live in their urban homes cannot help but affect it quite profoundly. The moral of Stroud's story has implications far beyond the American Northeast: the region has forests today because people made choices about them and then did the hard practical and political work of making those choices real. Such things do not happen by accident. They happen because people make them happen. That is as true today as it was a hundred years ago.

Acknowledgments

This book was only possible because of the generosity of many friends, relatives, colleagues, advisors, teachers, mentors, students, librarians, archivists, neighbors, and strangers. I want to thank everyone who had a hand in shaping the work and in seeing that I completed it, even though it will be impossible to name them all.

My first debts as an historian are to Daniel Pope and Louise Wade at the University of Oregon, who were my mentors as I began graduate work. I had so many mentors, colleagues, and friends at Oregon: Arne Buechling asked questions and told stories that led me to this topic; John Van Sant pushed me to take risks; Killian Barefoot, Colleen Broderick, Amy Fulwyler, Weijing Lu, Heather Miller, and Douglas Seefeldt taught me that academia could be fun.

Kenneth T. Jackson, Eric Foner, Elliott Sclar, and especially Elizabeth Blackmar at Columbia University saw me through the dissertation years and the early drafts of what eventually became this book, and my classmates Martha S. Jones and Christopher Capozzola never stopped insisting that I finish what I had begun. New York City became home and the Ph.D. possible because of the tremendous support of many people, including Caroline Bynum, Cathleen Cahill, Jaye Fox, Mike Fuquay, Mary Gaines, Emily Gaines-Tecchio, Eagle Glassheim, Sara Gregg, Chris Herlinger, Molly Laird, Neil Maher, Keith O'Brien, Adrienne Petty, Leo Quigley, Guenther Roth, Andrew Sandoval-Strausz, Zachary Schrag, Mick Stevens, Ashli White, Ellen Wurtzel, Wendy Urban-Mead, and Marcia Wright.

I am also grateful to my colleagues, students, and friends at Oberlin College, especially Lisa Abend, Heidi Adelman, Radhika Atit, Heidi Ballard, Jennifer Bryan, Anna Gade, Meredith Gadsby, Katy Janda, Peter Kalliney, Manish Mehta, Beth Mitchell, Pablo Mitchell, Laura Moore, Charles Peterson, Karen Rignall, Debbie Schildkraut, Andy Shanken, and Anne Trubek. I am particularly grateful for the support of the History Department, the members of which mentored and supported me in countless ways. Friends and colleagues at the University of Michigan and Ohio State University also offered invaluable support during my years in the Midwest; Heather Miller from Oregon and Martha Jones from Columbia were once again close by; they continued to read and critique this work and to cook and eat with me, which mattered. Rob Genter and John Carson pushed me forward and supported me at critical junctures as well.

My move to Bryn Mawr College came at a crucial moment for me. Within months of my return to my hometown of Philadelphia, my sixty-four-year-old father was diagnosed with stage-four prostate cancer. My then very new friends and colleagues at Bryn Mawr made it possible for me to continue writing and keep sane as I accompanied my dad through the final two years of his life and then mourned his passing. I am very grateful to Kim Cassidy, Yvie Fabella, John Griffith, Lori Griffith, Kathy Izumi, Gary McDonogh, Terry McLaughlin, Chris Oze, Katherine Rowe, Jamie Taylor, Bryn Thompson, Nate Wright, and Gretchen Wright for helping me navigate a devastating three years. Bryn shepherded me through the most challenging six weeks of my academic career, and I can't thank her enough. My parents' Heyward Street neighbors and their good friends from Bala also deserve special thanks, and Beth Bailey, Duncan Black, David DiSabatino, Michelle Jacoby, Thom Kriner, Warren Liu, Terri McNamara, Jen Roder, Bethany Schneider, Zachary Schrag, Rosi Song, Mayumi Takada, Kate

Thomas, Sharon Ullman, Juliet Whelan, Ashli White, Lauren Winner, and my Iseminger Street neighbors all helped me through that time in ways both big and small.

My students at Bryn Mawr also deserve special mention; their enthusiasm, intellect, and creativity keep me hopping. Likewise, I am indebted to my colleagues in the Tri-Co Environmental Studies Program, and also to Nan Harris for her support of the college, its students, the Environmental Studies Program, and my own research. I am honored to hold the Johanna Alderfer Harris and William H. Harris, M.D., Chair in Environmental Studies at Bryn Mawr.

From my first years as a graduate student, I have been welcomed, challenged, encouraged, supported, and pushed by a great many colleagues across the field of environmental history. Richard White offered early encouragement and Bill Cronon saw me through at the end. Drew Isenberg, Matt Klingle, Neil Maher, Kathy Morse, and especially Ari Kelman kept me going through the treacherous middle. Kathleen Brosnan, Connie Chiang, Tom Dunlap, Sarah Elkind, Susan Ferber, Mark Fiege, Sara Gregg, Richard Judd, Nancy Langston, Martin Melosi, Linda Nash, Sara Pritchard, Harriet Ritvo, Christopher Sellers, Jeffrey Stine, Joel Tarr, Jay Taylor, and Louis Warren have all taught me a great deal, as have so many other members of the American Society for Environmental History. The society has been an important intellectual home for me, and I am grateful to executive director Lisa Mighetto for all she does to make that true.

In addition to intellectual and financial support from the University of Oregon, Columbia University, Oberlin College, and Bryn Mawr College, my work on this project has received direct and indirect support from many agencies, organizations, and institutions. A graduate fellowship from the U.S. Environmental Protection Agency's "Science to Achieve Results (STAR)" program funded my final years of graduate study, and a grant from the Pennsylvania Historical and Museum Commission supported my work as well. In addition, an American Council of Learned Societies Andrew W. Mellon Junior Faculty Fellowship provided crucial time for writing.

During my year as an ACLS Mellon Junior Faculty Fellow, I also had the support of Harvard University's Charles Warren Center for Studies in American History. As part of that year's seminar on the Culture and Politics of the Built Environment in North America, led by Lizabeth Cohen and Margaret Crawford, I learned a tremendous amount from our group: Daniel Abramson, Eric Avila, Alice Friedman, Paul Groth, Jane Kamensky, Paula Lupkin, Martha McNamara, and Anne Whiston Spirn. In addition to my Warren Center colleagues, Christopher Capozzola, David Ciarlo, Jack Dennerlein, Chris Herlinger, Keith O'Brien, Barbara Savage, Ned Welch, and Tiziana Casciaro all made that year a particularly productive and important one.

I had the privilege of a residential fellowship year again more recently, this time at the National Humanities Center in North Carolina, where I was supported by a fellowship funded by the National Endowment for the Humanities (which also means that I am contractually obligated to point out that "any views, findings, conclusions or recommendations expressed in this book do not necessarily reflect those of the National Endowment for the Humanities." Nothing here should be taken as the view of any organization or of any person other than myself, and while *Nature Next Door* has been improved in many ways by the advice, critiques, and corrections of others, all errors are my own).

My NEH-supported year at the National Humanities Center was a transformative time for me and for this book. Colleagues there and the staff at the center supported my work on both this project and others in quite profound ways, and I am deeply grateful in particular to fellow scholars Mia Bay, Joe Boone, Chad Bryant, Jared Farmer, Jack P. Greene, Michael Kulikowski, Tom Lekan, Magda Maczynska, Beth Quitslund, and David Schoenbrun; housemate and colleague extraordinaire Lauren F. Winner; copyediting wizard Karen Carroll; librarian superstars Josiah Drewry, Jean Houston, and Eliza Robertson; and the entire National Humanities Center staff, especially Marie Brubaker, Kent Mullikin, Sarah Payne, Pat Schreiber, and Don Solomon.

Dozens of librarians and archivists throughout the Northeast have been critical to my completing this project, and I wish I could name them all. I am particularly grateful to Linda Shopes, who was extremely helpful to me during my time in residence at the Pennsylvania Historical and Museum Commission and after, as were Linda Ries and Michael Sherbon. Among the many helpful librarians at Bryn Mawr College, Andrew Patterson stands out for having tracked down multiple obscure sources in the depths of the collection when deadlines loomed. Paul Carnahan at the Vermont Historical Society, Roland Goodbody at the University of New Hampshire Library's Milne Special Collections, and Dani Fazio of the Maine Historical Society went far beyond anything I could have hoped for in helping me track down images, as did Cheryl Oakes and Eben Lehman of the Forest History Society. In addition to Cheryl and Eben, I am grateful to the Forest History Society's entire staff for their support.

I am also indebted to Marianne Keddington-Lang, acquisitions editor for the University of Washington Press. From very early conversations when this project was still taking shape until she coaxed me into letting go of the manuscript many too many years later, she has helped me make this not just a better book, but a book. Copyeditor Jeanne Ponzetti caught more errors than I thought I had left for her, and managing editor Marilyn Trueblood and designer Thomas Eykemans brought everything together expertly during the final steps. I am grateful to each of them and to the entire staff of the press.

Rachel Hope Allison created the beautiful maps; her patience with my changing ideas and deadlines was almost as remarkable as her skill as an artist. She always found time to work with me, even as she was on deadline for her own book, a fabulous graphic novel about the Great Pacific Garbage Patch, *I am Not a Plastic Bag* (Los Angeles: Archaia, 2012).

I also want to acknowledge two publications in which I have told portions of stories that are also found here. Olive Cousins and her experiences on E Plantation in Maine from chapter 4 of *Nature Next Door* also play a role in my essay "Who Cares About Forests? How Forest History Matters," in *A Companion to Environmental History*, ed. Douglas Sackman, 41–42 (West Sussex, UK: Wiley-Blackwell, 2010). Mira Dock's work for Pennsylvania's forests, from chapter 1, appears in somewhat different form in my essay "Urban Environmental History in Mid-Atlantic City," in the Fall 2012 issue of *Pennsylvania History*, a special issue on the Environmental History of the Mid-Atlantic region, edited by Allen Dieterich-Ward and David Hsiung, with journal editor Bill Pencak. I want to thank the editors and the presses for their support of my work.

Finally, this book could never have been completed without the support of my family. My sister Beth Stroud and her partner Chris Paige have both read multiple drafts of this book; they and my sister Mary (whom everyone else calls Max) have never flagged in their support of my work, even when it seemed like the project would never come to an end. Heather Johnston, Heather Miller, and Yvie Fabella I count as family as well, and I know they are as happy as Beth, Chris, and Mary to see this book finally done, as are all of the cousins and aunts who have been hearing about this project for far too long. And I owe a special thanks to Michael Kulikowski, who has made it all fun again.

Because this project took so long, there were people who saw its beginnings but are not here to see its end. In addition to my father, I wish I were able to share this work with my grandfather J. W. Bigham, my grandmother Marion Stroud, my father's brothers, Joe and George Stroud, my student Hans Petersen, and my childhood friend Liz Whithed Boyson, all of whom I miss. But this book is not only about the past but also about hopes for the future, which is why I have dedicated it to the memory of my father, Bill Stroud, and to my mother, Jamie Stroud, as well as to their grandchildren, my nieces and nephew: Nevaeh Williams Paige, Connor Henson-Stroud, and Ruby Henson-Stroud. I hope they will all enjoy the woods as much as my father did, and for many more years.

A Note on the Maps

The forest cover maps and reforestation statistics in this volume draw on data from multiple sources, the most important of which are Charles S. Sargent's *Report on the Forests of North America (exclusive of Mexico), Tenth Census of the United States, 1880* (Washington, D.C.: Government Printing Office, 1884) and the U.S. Forest Service's National Forest Inventory and Analysis (FIA) Databases, accessible through the "Forest Inventory Data Online (FIDO) system, at http://apps.fs.fed.us/fido. Additional information for each of the individual states draws on both the secondary sources and the federal and state forest surveys and reports that are cited in the endnotes.

The maps and statistics presented here should be understood as illustrative, not as numerical representations of precise changes in numbers of trees, since methods of gathering and expressing information about forest cover have changed dramatically since 1880, when Charles Sargent wrote to local officials across the country, asking them to estimate the extent of forests in their counties. Also, since early information on the extent of forest cover was most often reported at the county level, the maps for both the early and the later years are based on county-level information. Artist Rachel Hope Allison translated the county-by-county data into works of art to convey the scale and scope of the changes in forest cover over the course of the twentieth century. The location maps in each of the chapters are her artwork as well.

Nature
Next Door

The City and the Trees

E very May, before the city heat became unbearable, Philadelphia lawyer Herbert Welsh packed a small backpack, a blanket, some snacks,
and his umbrella and headed off from his fashionable neighborhood
in Germantown for a five-hundred-mile walk to New Hampshire. In late
June he arrived at his family's summer house at Lake Sunapee, ready for a
season's work of campaigning to protect the forests of the Northeast.

Welsh made his first trek in 1915, at the age of sixty-four, and repeated it
annually well into his seventies. Along his way, he ate simple dinners with
tramps and slept in fields; other nights, he dined with Yale faculty and retired
to well-appointed guestrooms. Over the years, Welsh made many friends
along his route, and they began to look for him each summer.

His first stop was always McCauley's Hotel in New Hope, Pennsylvania, a thirty-mile walk from Germantown. In order to reach McCauley's in
time for afternoon tea on the lawn by the Delaware River, he had to leave
Germantown at four in the morning. A week later, he would arrive at his
daughter's apartment at Seventy-second Street and Lexington Avenue in
Manhattan, where a skeptical doorman would announce his arrival. Continuing north, he stopped to visit friends, acquaintances, and strangers. New

1.1 Herbert Welsh on his way from Philadelphia to Lake Sunapee, New Hampshire, in the early twentieth century. The Historical Society of Pennsylvania, Herbert Welsh Collection [0702], Photos Box 1.

Haven, Northampton, Brattleboro, and camps and lodges in between were annual rest stops on the way to Sunapee, where he was joined by his wife, children, grandson, and servants. They preferred to travel by train.

In his memoir of the walks, Welsh explained that he undertook his journey to commune with nature and appreciate the wildness of the region. What he most enjoyed was the chance to shed the worries and concerns of the city, to purge himself of the year's work behind a desk, and to arrive in Sunapee a cleansed man, a creature of the woods. Yet despite his rhetoric and illusions, he was never far from town on his long walk through the northeastern forest, and he rarely suffered for company, refreshment, or—when he chose to look for them—a roof and a featherbed. Despite his desire to get closer to nature, Welsh was hardly in the wilderness.[1] He was traveling through a continuous, populated region in which both wildness and his beloved trees were new.

Although historians and historical actors alike have often understood urban and rural areas as distinct, they are fundamentally intertwined, and nowhere more so than in the northeastern United States. As Herbert Welsh experienced so keenly on his summer treks, twentieth-century northeastern farms, forests, agriculture, industry, nature, and culture had become part of a single transformed regional landscape. Both cities and trees—the region's burgeoning urban centers and the accompanying new forests that had only recently taken root—bound the whole place together.

A twentieth-century upsurge in acreage of forested land seems counterintuitive at first, especially in a region of tremendous urbanization and population growth. But the statistics tell a striking story. In the late nineteenth century, 25 percent of New York State was forested; by the late twentieth century, the figure was 61 percent. Likewise, forest cover in Vermont increased from 35 to 76 percent, and in New Hampshire, from 50 to 86 percent. Today, the northeastern United States is almost 75 percent forested.[2] Changes in land management, ownership patterns, and ideas about forests and trees that emerged in Welsh's day are what made that new forest possible at a time when cities, too, were growing. The region's dramatic reforestation blossomed in step with an urban boom.

I am using "reforestation" here as Herbert Welsh would have used the term, to refer to the return of trees, however they came back. Professional foresters would quibble with this terminology: "afforestation" would be their preferred word, understanding "reforested" land as only those acres actively planted with trees. Yet Welsh and his contemporaries, like much of the general public today, frequently had little sense of how it was that trees returned. Nevertheless, they knew well that fields had become forests, and those forests were to be cherished and saved.

Men and women like Welsh believed it would take their hard work and dedication to safeguard the future of these new trees and see the forested acreage grow. Welsh and many of his colleagues and friends were city residents with a love of the outdoors and an intellectual fascination with the workings of the natural world, and they enjoyed the forest as a landscape of leisure. But beyond such selfish motives, Welsh and other forest advocates

NORTHEASTERN UNITED STATES

1.2   The northeastern United States. Map by Rachel Hope Allison.

believed that city and country life were connected—intellectually, perhaps spiritually, and definitely physically. The wooded land beyond Philadelphia's borders guaranteed city people space for recreation, clean air to breathe, wood for timber and fuel, and pure water to drink. For Welsh and others like him, re-creating and protecting the region's forests was a vital urban concern.

By the time Herbert Welsh began his walks that summer in 1915, he had come to think of Sunapee, New York City, Philadelphia, and all of the forests and rivers and farms in between as part of a single landscape in which he had a deep personal interest.[3] And though there had long been strong ties between the cities of the Northeast and their hinterlands, Welsh's experience was new. Urban growth, changes in the northeastern economy, and the new science of forestry had all brought cities and the countryside much closer together, both materially and in thought. The forests of New Hampshire now seemed—and for Welsh, were—a mere stroll from Germantown.

Ever since trains had begun bringing western grain to eastern cities in the nineteenth century, northeastern farmers had been finding it harder to sell what they grew. As farmers struggled, turning to other pursuits or moving to farms farther west, forests were quick to encroach on their abandoned fields.[4] At the same time, populations were booming in New York City, Philadelphia, Boston, Manchester, and other northeastern cities and towns, placing new demands on the region's land and resources. By the end of the century, scientifically trained foresters were joining urban activists, nature enthusiasts, agricultural organizations, investors, and state politicians in the debate over how best to craft and preserve the forested landscape that Welsh and his contemporaries considered so vital for the region and that northeasterners continue to enjoy today. Some of these people were most interested in cultivating lumber for urban markets; others in creating parks for urban tourists; still others in crafting upriver forests as protective buffers for cities' drinking water supplies. Cities and forests, as Welsh understood, were connected. The cities could kill off the forests and suffer for it, or they could foster the growth of trees.

Because of decisions Welsh and his contemporaries made, the forests did very well. Growing cities, changes in farming, booming tourism, shifts in the timber industry, and new ideas about the uses and functions of trees

have together brought about and secured a robust northeastern woods: this region of fifty million people is also home to seemingly endless acres of trees. It didn't have to be so, and yet it is: cities and forests grew together. If we want to understand how people and forests can live together—rather than competing, to the impoverishment of both—then the Northeast has much to teach us.

The story of forests returning to the region is partly one of ecology. It is hard to keep the trees away, even though many people have tried very hard to do just that, clearing land for agriculture, for homes, and for factories. The reforestation story is also one of technology, transportation, and complex economies. Trees were only able to reclaim the Northeast once people there could import much of their food from elsewhere. And it is, finally, a story of persistent effort on the part of forest advocates, who sometimes had great and acknowledged successes and many times were successful despite policies later regarded as misguided and ill-informed. Foresters and other promoters of woods did not always accomplish what they set out to do, and the results of their policies were not always what they expected, but their actions helped shape the landscape that is the forested Northeast of today. The trees returned, and the entire region was reshaped, as part of a complex relationship between nature and people who had designs on the land.

The symbiotic relationship between twentieth-century northeastern cities and their neighboring woods upsets the common understanding that as cities

1.3   A work crew planting seedlings in New York State in the early twentieth century. Handwriting on the back of the photograph reads "Planting seedlings in an old pasture without breaking the ground." Forest History Society Image Collection Folder "Reforestation—Planting, Hand 1/3." Courtesy of the Forest History Society.

1.4   A more formal-looking group of men planting a northeastern woodlot in the early twentieth century. The handwritten note on the back of this image describes "a gang at work planting young pines in an opening made by cutting out the chestnut timber. Some are using dibbles instead of grubbing hoes." An additional typewritten note adds that the group is "probably a Yale School of Forestry class doing field work. 1915?" Forest History Society Image Collection Folder "Reforestation—Planting, Hand 1/3." Courtesy of the Forest History Society.

grow, they necessarily strip resources from surrounding territory, domesticating landscapes for miles around. Cities, the historiography tells us, are consumers, not creators, of nature. In many places, that narrative has been true. Chicago grew as it fed off the forests of the Midwest, for example, developing in tandem with a sprawling farmscape that tamed nature throughout the region.[5] Processes of urbanization—fueled by advances in technology, transportation, and agriculture—stripped Chicago's hinterland of natural resources. Yet as those changes were happening in Chicago and its hinterland, they offered a period of recovery for land to the east.

My focus on the urban role in creating and maintaining the new northeastern forests joins that of many urban environmental historians in emphasizing the interrelatedness of natural and cultural landscapes and the implausibility of separating the two. Frequently, those interactions have been characterized as one-sided: the only possible urban role is that of degradation of nature. But in the early twentieth-century Northeast, interactions between city and hinterland went in both directions, creating a new wildness of metropolitan nature: a reforested landscape intricately entangled with the region's cities. By focusing on this urban contribution to the creation of the forests, I challenge the anti-urban bias and the cliché of environmental decline that pervade so many environmental stories. By doing so, I illustrate the centrality of social processes in the production of the seemingly wild landscapes of the White Mountains, the Allegheny National Forest, and the many wooded lands in between.[6]

Nature Next Door centers on the period between 1890 and 1930, when state governments of the Northeast—together with federal and local agencies, conservationists, scientists, civic activists, farmers, industrialists, and laborers—were actively thinking about and working toward creating and managing new forests. Their legacy includes not only greater public land holdings, but also tree nurseries, forestry schools, forestry commissions and agencies, and many acres of new trees. Decisions made during those years created the mosaic of laws and land holdings that have made the forests of today a reality and that frame the possibilities for their future.

The history of northeastern farmers abandoning their hilly and rocky lands for western farms and eastern cities is a familiar one, but there is more to learn about the land left behind. The return of forest to former farmland and other cutover tracts is not merely the result of benign neglect, allowing forests to establish themselves wherever they were no longer beaten back to make space for fields. Trees came back because time and ecology gave them favor, but they were also encouraged and protected by choice.[7]

And the new forest is not monolithic; it has returned in different ways and shapes in response to conditions that vary among the states, including settlement patterns, planting programs, preservation campaigns, tax policies, industrial development, and the tourist business. Private hunting grounds differ wildly from watershed lands, which are different still from timber plantations and public parks. But almost all of the trees are new and connected in some way to cities nearby.

The story of dramatic reforestation can also obscure as much as it reveals. More trees and more animals do not necessarily mean greater biodiversity or a healthier environment. Many suburbs have more trees than the farmland they replaced, but they also have more pavement, more cars, and more pollution. "Reforestation" is both a material and a cultural term, and the definition of "forest" has changed over time as well. There is little agreement among historians, ecologists, professional foresters, or the general public as to what justifies the label "forest," much less the point at which we can consider a formerly treeless tract of land "reforested."

Walking through a forest, one rarely pauses to ask "why is this a forest?" or "what is it that makes this place count, and another not?" Those questions matter. "Forest" has meant different things to different people, and we must pay attention to what people thought they were talking about when they spoke of forested land. They have not always meant what we think they have. Sometimes their perceptions matched the physical landscapes; other times they did not. There are nuanced relationships among language, perception, and changes in the physical landscape, and those relationships have shaped decisions about managing the land. The result has been a mosaic of forested landscapes throughout the Northeast. The forests of suburban Philadelphia are different from the forests of the Green Mountains, which are distinct from those of northern Maine. Each forest reflects its own history and ecology, and yet we can speak of all three places as forested—and as reforested.

The many forests vary in size, age, diversity, coherence, and function, but they also differ dramatically in the trees themselves: there is not and never has been a single northeastern woods. The region's abundant rainfall, favorable soils, moderate climate, and decent if not extensive growing season all mean that undisturbed land is rarely without trees for long, though the forest composition can vary a great deal. Over a hundred different kinds of trees are at home in the Northeast, with different species tending to dominate as you travel north. Minor differences in soils, elevation, wind patterns, hill slope, and shade also influence which trees dominate a particular area, with land use history and local forest management programs having dramatic effects as well.[8]

Much of the Northeast is cloaked in hardwoods—commonly beech, yellow birch, and sugar maple, mixed with hemlock, sweet birch, red maple, and black cherry. On sandier soils, white pines or oak trees take over, with oak trees far more common farther south. In cooler areas to the north, in swampy places, and at higher elevations, spruce, fir, and cedar are more common. The tree communities are related and can replace one another over time. Pine, spruce, and fir, for example, all need shade to survive their first few years. So after logging or fire in a spruce and fir region, hardwoods generally predominate, until spruce and fir get firmly established and crowd out the hardwoods. Pine trees do not generally win in competition with hardwoods, since they need abundant light to thrive after surviving their first years. With their thick bark, however, pine trees are very resistant to fire. When fire strikes a mixed stand of hardwoods and pines, the pines are often left standing. Just as these northeastern forests have played muse to generations of nature writers and ecologists, so foresters and visitors can read the history of these landscapes from the mixtures of species, ages, and conditions of the trees.[9]

The dramatic changes in forest communities that result from logging, fire, thinning, and shade mean that there are many distinct northeastern forests, despite the apparent ecological coherence of the region. The differences are not solely the result of human actions, but neither are they merely artifacts

1.5 "A pine forest follows a fire in New York, 1900," reads the notation on the back of this photograph. Thick bark makes pine trees particularly resistant to fire. Forest History Society Image Collection Folder "Reforestation—Natural, East and South 5/6." Courtesy of the Forest History Society.

of nature. The many woodlands that took root in the region from 1890 to 1930 were remarkably varied, and the people of each state—faced with different political and economic circumstances—brought back different trees.

Much of the writing on changes in northeastern land use emphasizes the city or the countryside, rather than the interaction between the two. Yet urbanization has had profound effects beyond urban boundaries, and changes in the countryside have shaped urban spaces as well. Reforestation has been most dramatic in an extraordinarily urban part of the nation. Interactions between the people and processes of northeastern cities and hinterlands have created this counterintuitive state.[10]

Furthermore, most scholarship on twentieth-century American forests has focused not on forests, but on forestry. And scholars studying forestry have looked primarily to the West, where the forest industry and the conservation movement have directed most of their energy and where the U.S.

Forest Service and the National Park Service have gained control of the most land.[11] The landscape changes of the East remain relatively underexplored.

There are, of course, notable exceptions, as both historians and policy analysts begin to focus their attention on the dramatic return of woods to the Northeast. Cities, however, have remained largely absent from most narratives. Despite the fact that northeastern cities and forests grew up together, writers who care deeply about forests, the environment, and environmental politics have most often cast urban centers as enemies of the woods.[12]

Cities are with us and are not going away, which means that we risk catastrophic distraction when we imagine them out of existence or wish urban populations onto family farms. We must understand how these sprawling urban places have grown with the new forests, so we can learn how best to nurture those positive connections and retain the rich landscapes of which forests and cities are both a part. Though northeastern forests and cities have flourished together over the past century, such has not been true everywhere and may cease to be true even in the Northeast. The region's history teaches us that healthy cities and rich forests can feed each other, but it is not necessarily so. We must pay attention to what worked.

We must also be careful not to be tempted by the apparent simplicity of the Northeast's ecological transformation. Some environmental writers have been seduced by the dramatic reforestation in the region, seeing it as evidence of nature's enormous regenerative potential and an argument against the notion that humans can damage the earth beyond repair. Others have tried to draw easy analogies between the Northeast and other deforested regions of the world, where ecologies, economies, and politics have created very different situations and management possibilities. But those who see the regrowth of the Northeast's forests as evidence of environmental progress that can be replicated anywhere fail to understand the specifics of time and place that lie behind the northeastern case. The ecology of New England and the Mid-Atlantic, the technology of transportation, and the position of the northeastern United States in the world economy have all contributed to the temporal and geographic specificity of the return of northeastern trees.[13]

Local politics matter as well. Environmental historians have made significant new contributions to understanding the past by deliberately putting nature at the center of their stories, showing how forests, rivers, grasslands, and wildlife pay little attention to human conventions like national boundaries and state lines. But this approach can sometimes obscure the significant impact that political structures have on natural systems. Municipal, state, and federal agencies and commissions have all played critical roles in bringing back northeastern forests, and have shaped them in different ways in each of the region's states. In understanding the diversity of northeastern forests, we can read American history through the trees.

When *New York Times* journalist Christopher Wren ushered in his retirement with a walk from Times Square in Manhattan to his summer home in Post Mills, Vermont, in 2001, he was sixty-five, a year older than Herbert Welsh was on his 1915 trek. Wren had far more company on his walk, since he spent many of his four hundred miles with fellow hikers along the Appalachian Trail, completed in 1937. And he faced many more hazards, too: dodging SUVs, jumping electric fences, searching for water in inhospitable suburban sprawl. Yet, like Welsh, he marveled at the new woods and at the stone walls that wound through them, reminders of the cleared fields that had once been in their place.[14]

The most surprising thing that Wren could tell his fellow hikers was that he had begun his hike at his office and that he had walked into the woods from Times Square. Young men and women who had begun their hikes in Georgia, over one thousand miles earlier than Wren's, couldn't imagine how the retired foreign correspondent could have begun hiking in Manhattan and found his way to the trees. Where Welsh and his contemporaries saw obvious connections between the urban and forested landscapes, today those connections are too often obscured and the landscapes seem to exist in isolation from one another. But Wren had it right: hiking from Times Square to the Green Mountain forest is not so strange. The cities and forests of the Northeast are all of a piece and place.[15]

CHAPTER ONE

Water and Woods
in Pennsylvania

Walking through the ancient hemlock grove in the bottom of a remote valley in Pennsylvania's Huntingdon County, hikers in the 1890s may have wondered why a patch of tall evergreens was still standing when nearly everything nearby had been cut down. This area in the south central part of the state is known as Seven Sisters, and by the end of the nineteenth century, each of the seven mountains from which its name derives had been sheared of trees. Only the valley floor remained green. Perhaps a property dispute between two lumber companies saved these few majestic acres. Or maybe the company that was cutting in the area went bankrupt before the final trees were down. No one seems to know for sure.[1]

While the hemlocks remain an unexplained anomaly and the most regal living things in sight, they no longer gaze on naked hills. They are surrounded by thousands of acres of hundred-year-old red oak, yellow birch, black birch, ash, cucumber magnolia, striped maple, sugar maple, basswood, tulip trees, sycamore, and rhododendron. The five-hundred-year-old hemlocks are ensconced in a rambling, messy, and beautiful eighty-thousand-acre state forest, a lush landscape of old trees that appears timeless, endless, and wild.[2]

It seems inevitable, this treed land. These mountainsides and riverbanks have always welcomed woods. Even when loggers cut with abandon, trees grew back easily and quickly. In areas where Pennsylvania's agricultural and mining industries were at their height in the early nineteenth century, saplings threatened to fill in fields and take back mill sites if vigilance lagged. It was constant work to fight back the forest. But by the end of the nineteenth century, it seemed as though this marvelously resilient landscape was nevertheless doomed. Too much had been cut too fast, and too thoroughly, for too long.

Ever since the early years of European settlement, farmers in Pennsylvania and throughout the Northeast had aggressively cleared forests to make way for fields. Even as the twentieth century dawned, property owners continued to harvest trees at a rapid rate, encouraged to clear as much land as possible by tax policies and lucrative markets for lumber and fuel. But as the state's cities grew and as scientists developed compelling theories about the role of forests in filtering water supplies and preventing both floods and drought, urban activists began to push for a more comprehensive understanding of the value of trees.

As we look back on nineteenth-century seedlings amidst tangles of vine, hindsight allows us to see a future of mature forests taking root in the ravaged landscape. We now know that the trees encroaching on recently abandoned farm, mining, and lumber land—if left alone—would become towering woodlands, a rich habitat for mammals, birds, insects, molds, flowers, fungi, and ferns. But the nineteenth-century hiker instead saw desolation, ruined industry, ill-managed land, and a threat of timber famine that would starve the region in more ways than one. Who would ensure that the land would, in fact, be left alone? The answer, it turns out, lay miles away, in the largest cities of the state.

Those fears of timber famine, drought, and disappearing jobs were keenly felt in the state capital in Harrisburg, in the industrial sectors of Pittsburgh, and throughout the scientific community in Philadelphia. As those cities grew, their residents pushed their municipal governments, their state legislators, and eventually the national government to create new forests and put

1.1 Along the Schuylkill River, Philadelphia, ca. 1870. R. Newell and Son. Philadelphia: Stereoscopic Views. P.9299.63 [detail]. Courtesy of the Library Company of Philadelphia.

1.2   A train trestle crosses cleared land at Kittaning Point in the Allegheny Mountains. Photograph by John Moran, 1831-1903. P.8992.17 [detail]. Courtesy of the Library Company of Philadelphia.

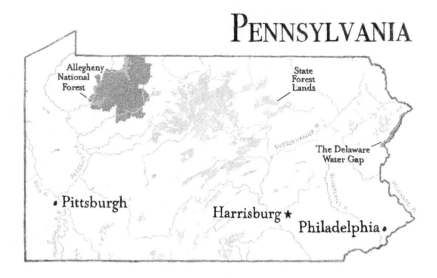

PENNSYLVANIA

Allegheny National Forest

State Forest Lands

SUSQUEHANNA R

The Delaware Water Gap

• Pittsburgh

Harrisburg ★

Philadelphia •

1.3   Important locations in Pennsylvania. Map by Rachel Hope Allison.

newly forested land under government protection to safeguard against future disaster.

The situation seemed dire. By the end of the nineteenth century, most of Pennsylvania's forests had been cleared for agriculture, mining, timber, and homes. Less than 40 percent of the state's territory could still be called "forest land," and for most of that, the term was a stretch. Almost all of the land had been cut over at least once, and where trees were left standing, they were frequently pathetic, tiny specimens. In a state that had been named for forests and had once been virtually blanketed in trees, Penn's woods had almost vanished.

Pennsylvanians fretted their loss. By the 1890s, beating back wilderness in the service of civilization no longer seemed wise. People were coming to believe—if haltingly—that they were dependent on environments much more complex than had seemed possible before. A region without trees, they were learning, would be bereft not only of lumber, fuel, and the income of a

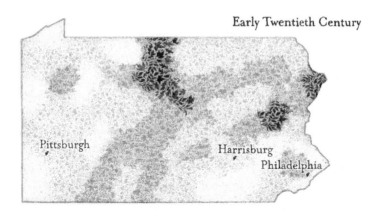

Early Twentieth Century

Pittsburgh

Harrisburg
Philadelphia

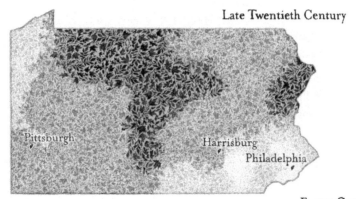

Late Twentieth Century

Pittsburgh

Harrisburg
Philadelphia

PENNSYLVANIA

Forest Cover

1 to 25%

26 to 50%

51 to 75%

76 to 100%

1.4 The increase in forest cover in Pennsylvania during the twentieth century.
Map by Rachel Hope Allison.

timber industry but also of drinking water, reliable water power, and navigable rivers. Trees, scientists of the day warned the state's citizens, regulated and purified the water of the state's rivers and reservoirs. Trees captured rainfall in soil, allowing water to filter slowly to rivers and lakes; leaves sheltered snow from the sun and moderated the speed at which ice and wintry drifts could melt; and forests even meant more rain, since trees coaxed moisture from the air by bringing the temperature down. Without forests, rain would splash across the hillsides' surfaces and race to rivers the moment it fell from the sky, plaguing the state with floods in the spring and droughts in the summer. And another danger loomed: water quality. Without forests as filters, drinking water would become foul.[3]

In an address to the state legislature in 1896, Pennsylvania Governor Daniel H. Hastings described his fear of a treeless future. "This is perhaps the first generation in this Commonwealth that has been brought face to face with the dangers and disasters of a timberless country," he told legislators. Even land classified as forest, he declared, "possesses almost nothing that is worthy of the name or would be valued by the lumberman for sale or by the mechanic for construction. Many of these large, unproductive tracts present a picture of desolation which cannot well be contemplated without awakening apprehension as to their future bearing on the prosperity of the Commonwealth." These sorry and desolate "woodlands," if not restored, would mean the loss of both timber income and lumber supply for the state.[4]

But the governor was most concerned about implications for the state's water supply. "It is recognized as a fact that of the waters which fall upon cleared areas, four-fifths are lost because they run immediately out of the country; while four-fifths of the waters which fall upon our forested areas are saved," he warned, quoting with confidence the newest understandings of how forests held water in the soil. "It is now submitted to the General Assembly that it would be both wise and profitable for the State, in some right manner, to become the owner of these vast and comparatively worthless forest areas which contain the source of our water supplies, and to hold them as such reservations, protecting them from forest fires and encouraging regrowth of forest timber."[5] It was a long struggle to get such lands under protection, and one that Hastings would not live to see fully realized, but his vision is now tangible in the 2.5 million acres of state and federally owned forests flourishing in Pennsylvania today. Many acres beyond that number are also in trees—privately held forests that state policy has both nurtured and protected.

Pennsylvania was the home of the nation's first professional forester; the site of the first state-run forest academy; an incubator of new scientific thought about the relationships between cities and trees; and ultimately a laboratory where ideas about taxes, forest management, urban beautification, and water supply were developed in ways that were later incorporated into land management policy throughout the nation. Pennsylvania—with its confusion of municipal structures (so different from the orderly townships of New England) and its unusual proliferation of large cities and towns (from Philadelphia to Scranton to Harrisburg to Pittsburgh and dozens of smaller places in between), combined with elite Philadelphians' sense of themselves as the leaders of the young republic's scientific community—was at the vanguard of managing wildlands and cities as part of one single, interdependent landscape.

That single landscape was clear to nineteenth-century observers like Governor Hastings and his contemporaries. Gifford Pinchot, who grew up in Milford, Pennsylvania, and whom Theodore Roosevelt appointed as the nation's first chief of the U.S. Forest Service in 1905, considered the connections between cities and distant landscapes to be self-evident. Joseph T. Rothrock, who took charge of the state's forests in 1893, saw safeguarding cities and towns as his primary job. Mira Dock, a botanist and city-beautiful activist from Harrisburg, who joined the state's Forestry Commission in 1901, had always connected the health of cities and their residents to the health and proliferation of trees.

Dependence on the natural world was much more tangible in a time when water was not available at the kitchen sink, and when sewage did not somehow magically disappear down drains or with the flush of a toilet. At the end of the eighteenth century, Philadelphia had just over 40,000 residents and—like every other city in the young country—no central water supply. People drew their water from private wells—often in a backyard, not far from the outhouse—or from local pumps. While scientists had not yet taken hold of germ theory to explain the spread of illness, most people associated foul-tasting water with disease. When a yellow fever epidemic swept the city in 1793 and again in 1798, city leaders came under serious pressure to make drinking water safe.[6]

In 1801, Philadelphia was both the largest American city and the first to build a municipal water supply system. Designed by engineer Benjamin Henry Latrobe, the system involved steam pumps at an intake station on the Schuylkill River to the city's west. The pumps brought water high enough out of the river to flow by gravity through wooden pipes to an elaborate building at Centre Square, where Philadelphia City Hall now stands. Inside the neoclassical building, another set of steam pumps pushed the water up to two water tanks enclosed in the top of the building. All Philadelphians able to pay a fee and build a connection to the main distribution pipes constructed throughout the city could have access to this river water from outside the built-up area, water that was believed to be more pure than any available from local wells.[7]

Despite being the newest and best thing at the time and a major sightseeing destination for visitors, within fifteen years the capacity and technology of the Centre Street Station were no longer sufficient. Latrobe's former assistant, Frederick Graff, designed and oversaw the construction of a complex of pumping stations on the east bank of the Schuylkill, along with a series of reservoirs atop the hill where the Philadelphia Art Museum now stands. That technology served the city for almost a century. The sophisticated waterworks were also beautifully landscaped, and both picnickers and engineers made the place a popular destination. By the mid-nineteenth century, over a hundred American cities had followed Philadelphia's example of providing water to their residents through municipal systems.[8]

As Philadelphians soon learned, however, providing centralized water and providing safe water, though connected, were not synonymous. As the city continued to grow, more sewage and other pollution from mills, factories, and homes entered the rivers upstream from Philadelphia faucets. In an effort to limit the pollution traveling from riverbanks to households, the Philadelphia city government began purchasing land along the Schuylkill River in 1843. In 1855, the city council formally named and dedicated the riverbank purchase areas as Fairmount Park, thereby establishing what would become one of the largest municipal parks in the country, encompassing 10 percent of the city's land. New York City's Central Park is a mere 843 acres; today, Fairmount Park totals over 9,000.[9]

The ideas behind the land purchases and the establishment of the park were simple and straightforward, and yet novel for their time. If there were no factories on the riverbanks, there would be no factory effluent to poison the water. If there were no homes lining the rivers, no household sewage would threaten the city's health. There was as yet little thought of trees or of forested upland watersheds being central to the safeguarding of water supplies; those ideas would be popularized later, most famously through the writings of George Perkins Marsh. At first, it was lack of development rather than presence of trees that caught the public imagination and seemed to promise water purity and public health.[10]

Because Philadelphia began early with water supply technology, it found itself on a path of technological dependence that meant its engineers and planners ultimately failed in what Boston and New York City were able to accomplish by beginning later, after the mistakes in Philadelphia were more fully understood. Those cities were able to protect their water supplies by controlling upriver land. Today, both Boston and New York City are able to offer their residents unfiltered drinking water because the forested lands surrounding their upstate reservoirs are protected and regulated to such an extent that chemical treatment alone is sufficient to ensure the water's safety. The U.S. Environmental Protection Agency closely monitors the water quality in those unfiltered reservoirs, and both cities one day soon may be forced to build filtration plants.[11]

Philadelphia, always on the cutting edge of water supply technology, began filtering all of its water in 1911, after failing to gain sufficient control over its upriver lands.[12] In failure, there was a different kind of success. Other municipalities looked to Philadelphia's experience, and thousands of acres of the state's lands were placed under protection in ways that would allow forests to return over the next century. Pennsylvanians changed the way that people in the region—urban residents, foresters, botanists, farmers, vacationers, and others—thought about the connections among cities, water, and trees. Though Philadelphia moved characteristically quickly to adopt a "modern" technological solution that would later look like giving up the good fight, the lessons learned there pointed toward more regional and ecological approaches to both land management and water supply security.

What had been modern in 1801 had become imperiled by the end of the century, prompting Governor Hastings's dire warnings of a treeless and parched future for the state. But it is precisely that century of striving to protect the Philadelphia water supply that brings us to Pennsylvania for the origins of the return of northeastern trees. Philadelphia was the nation's center of science, and it was in Philadelphia that the most dramatic advances were made in both water supply technology and understanding forests. Unfortunately, the strides made in the two fields were out of sync, and it was left to other large cities to build on what Philadelphia had learned. Because of advances made in Pennsylvania, New York and Boston were able to build their water supply systems with a clearer understanding of the role that forests could play.

The hydrology of forests, the technology of water supplies, the biology of particular trees—these were all new and exciting fields of inquiry in the nineteenth century, pursued by men of science (and a handful of women) who were not troubled by specialization in the same ways that we are today. In the nineteenth century, scientific disciplines—like landscapes—were understood as intertwined. Just as it was common sense for a city dweller of 1800 to feel dependent on distant lands for food, for water, and for resources of all kinds, it seemed sensible for an engineer to consider both medicine and botany as within his purview. All fell under the rubrics of natural philosophy and natural history; the study of how things worked and why—of understanding the world—all seemed of a piece.[13]

Benjamin Latrobe, the engineer of the Philadelphia waterworks, was a colleague of Benjamin Smith Barton, author of the first botanical textbook in the United States and professor of medicine at the University of Pennsylvania. They lived and worked in a city devoted to science and the natural world—a city that had been home to John Bartram (1699–1777) and his son William (1739–1823), leading naturalists of their day.[14]

Philadelphia was the city that hosted the young country's most important museums of nature. The American Philosophical Society, founded in 1743, was a society devoted principally to "natural philosophy," or understanding the way the world worked in both biological and intellectual ways. The Academy of Natural Sciences was founded in 1812 as a center devoted specifically to advancements in the study of what was then called "nature" in the broadest sense. A few years later, in 1824, the Franklin Institute was founded to showcase the newest technologies of the time. In 1858 the Mutter Museum of the College of Physicians of Philadelphia joined these institutions in their devotion to the study of the natural world and the spread of new understandings of science among the educated classes.[15]

It was in this milieu that Philadelphians beyond the scientific elite began to think about connections among forests, water, and health, reflecting a broad shift in American thinking about nature in the mid- to late nineteenth century. For the first time, onlookers began to equate purity and wildness with a natural, healthy order—an order threatened by the rapid changes and demands of cities bursting with new residents who needed clean water, clean streets, and freedom from disease-causing filth.

In nineteenth-century Philadelphia, a generation of elite and highly educated urban reformers and forest advocates had grown up intimately familiar with the Hudson River School painters, the transcendentalist writers Ralph Waldo Emerson and Henry David Thoreau from Massachusetts, and Vermonter George Perkins Marsh's landmark 1864 book, *Man and Nature; or, Physical Geography as Modified by Human Action*. The Hudson River School painters of the early and mid-nineteenth century in particular were part of a movement that idealized the American landscape and lamented its transformation and the loss of what they thought of as a pristine nature. Like those artists, Thoreau and contemporary authors romanticized a lost landscape and advocated interactions with nature that acknowledged human beings as a small part of a larger world, with nonhuman nature having value intrinsic to itself, beyond its utilitarian functions. And Marsh foretold of the devastation that would befall Americans if they failed to understand and respect the workings of the natural world.[16]

A lawyer, businessman, diplomat, and farmer, Marsh had traveled in the Mediterranean, and his observations there had convinced him that impending deforestation of his home state of Vermont and of the United States as a whole would lead to ruin.[17] He emphasized the interconnectedness of natural systems and man's heavy hand in manipulating nature beyond its ability to rebound. His writings on the relationships between forests and everything from fish populations to urban water supplies to human physical and economic health greatly influenced thinkers of his day.[18]

As Marsh was encouraging policy makers and timber developers to consider the broad effects of their actions, forest cover in the East was nearing its lowest ebb. At the same time, with new transportation technologies and the rapid development of the American West, more forests were becoming easily accessible and, therefore, more threatened. Many Americans' thoughts were turning to preserving the remaining trees.

As the natural world seemed to be retreating in the face of settlement and industrial development, advocates of preserving nature in its "wild" state were gaining a strong and popular following. In 1875, forest advocates organized the American Forestry Association. Sportsmen concerned with wildlife habitat, urban reformers thinking about the health benefits of parks and wilderness, farmers seeking greater productivity from their land, and industrialists wanting to protect supplies of natural resources were all part of a diverse population that was both receptive to and active in shaping new lines of thought about the proper use of land and resources in the United States.[19]

While the nineteenth-century study of forests and the engineering of water supply systems were generally undertaken by men, women's interest in natural history, botany, and forestry helped to popularize the new scientific understandings of connections among forests, water, and human health. Such concerns brought many women into the emerging conversation, and their interests pushed the direction of scientific inquiry. In the early to mid-nineteenth century, society women's interest in new scientific theories encouraged intellectual connections between urban home and country retreat, and between urban centers and forested lands. When the men who founded the American Academy of Natural Sciences in Philadelphia in 1812 needed to raise money to build their museum, they turned to local women and their seemingly more prosaic interests in order to raise the crucial funds. The men needed a place to house the rocks, shells, dead birds, and other specimens they were collecting, cataloguing, and categorizing in the name of a more complete understanding of nature, and society women had the money and the passion to help.[20]

The academy's most successful fund-raising campaign was centered on lectures attended by women who were more interested in the daily applications of the new scientific understandings than they were in taxonomy. Most of them cared less about the artifacts that had been divided, named, and counted than what the knowledge thereby gained could tell them about planning their gardens or understanding their parks and yards. "I am glad to hear that your Philadelphia damsels are indulging their taste in Botany," wrote Samuel Latham Mitchell, a New Yorker with an interest in the academy. "It will be a charming employment for those whose situation in life likens them to the lilies of the valley."[21] But these women took their education more seriously than Latham seems to have imagined. At the substantial sum of ten dollars for a series of tickets, women repeatedly filled the lecture halls, with implications for the future of botany and forests in Pennsylvania and beyond. These women and their daughters and granddaughters expanded the audience and market for scientific thought, pushing men to think harder about the systems of which their specimens were a part and to speak more effectively to an audience that was not scientifically trained.[22]

By the 1880s, European-educated foresters were bringing new emphases on economics to American forest work. In 1886 President Grover Cleveland appointed Bernard Fernow the third chief of the U.S. Department of Agriculture's Division of Forestry, which had been created in 1881. Fernow, who had been educated at the Prussian Forest Academy, brought with him a focus on the economic importance of the lumber industry and a keen interest in the science of forestry. In 1891, under Fernow's watch, fears about deforestation and its attendant problems of timber shortages, economic instability, flood, drought, and erosion prompted Congress to authorize the creation of forest reserves, later renamed national forests.[23]

Pennsylvanian Gifford Pinchot, who had been educated in France, took over as chief of the division in 1898 and became the nation's first chief of the U.S. Forest Service when it was created in 1905. By that time, a new generation of American foresters was being educated in European ideas about scientific management of forests in newly established technical forestry schools at Yale and Cornell, at Biltmore on the Vanderbilt estate in North Carolina, and at the Pennsylvania State Forest Academy at Mount Alto. National forest policy under Pinchot emphasized not preservation but rational use, based on new understandings of the functions and interrelations of soils, trees, and water.[24]

The conservationist ideal of rational use by no means displaced older ideas of preservation. Ideas of the judicious use of resources had informed Thomas Cole, Henry David Thoreau, and George Perkins Marsh, and ideas about the aesthetic and intrinsic value of forests informed many professional foresters. At the end of the nineteenth century, however, scientific conservation, not aesthetic preservation, dominated federal policy. It was from science and the dictates of practicality that forest advocates drew their authority.[25]

By the late nineteenth century, there was a general consensus both popularly and within the scientific community that forested watersheds had a tremendous influence on rivers, though there were divergent ideas about the precise mechanisms involved. Marsh and many of his contemporaries, for example, believed that forests literally created rain. They thought that by increasing air temperature and by providing windbreaks that captured clouds, trees attracted and created precipitation.[26] Such beliefs persisted in the popular imagination, though trained foresters at the end of the nineteenth century were beginning to reject them. Foresters pointed to other arguments, still largely accepted today, that trees in a river's watershed influenced water levels and water quality by controlling erosion and by holding precipitation in the soil, thereby moderating stream flow and reducing the chances of both flooding in the spring and drought in the summer. In addition, they pointed out, tree cover slowed the melting of snow, which also reduced the risk of flood. And, not inconsequentially, protecting forest preserves along rivers kept the pollution associated with industry and settlement away from vital water sources, as those early Philadelphians had figured out.[27]

Protecting water supplies was particularly difficult in Pennsylvania because of the convoluted and overlapping jurisdictions peculiar to the state. By the nineteenth century, the state had sixty-seven counties, which were home to over 2,500 cities, towns, townships, boroughs, and villages. In contrast to New England, Pennsylvania's county governments wielded and continue to wield significant power, and their jurisdiction over the collection of property taxes in the late nineteenth and early twentieth century was a significant factor in the creation of the state's forest system. As the twentieth century loomed, Governor Hastings and his contemporaries were gaining momentum in their fight to preserve, protect, and create woodlands throughout the state. Much of the land that would eventually become state forest was owned by county governments, which had seized it from individuals and corporations for nonpayment of taxes.[28]

And so, Pennsylvania's earliest efforts at reforestation of watersheds were complex, most often beginning at the municipal level, in negotiation with the counties and the state. By the 1880s Philadelphia doctors, among others, were worried that the Fairmount Park project, laudable though it was, would not be sufficient to keep the city's water pure. Charles M. Cresson, a chemist with Philadelphia's Board of Health, warned in 1886 that "as a lasting and effectual protection to the water supply the establishment of the Park has not proved a success." Population had risen too sharply within the watershed, he argued, and industries along the river beyond the boundaries of the park were presenting threats of contamination. Cresson argued that for the park project to be successful, "exclusive control must be had of the land upon both banks of the river for many miles above the city." To be able to protect its water supply, the city needed to control land beyond its borders.[29]

In 1893, a spreading cholera epidemic compelled panicked Philadelphians, already worried about typhoid, to band together with residents of other cit-

1.5 Ice houses along the Schuylkill River in Philadelphia, being demolished to make way for the expansion of Fairmount Park, ca. 1870. Photograph by Robert Newell, 1822-97. P.9061.33. Courtesy of the Library Company of Philadelphia.

ies to lobby for increased monitoring of municipal water supplies and to explore possibilities for other, more remote, and thus presumably purer water sources. Women's clubs, boards of trade, chambers of commerce, engineers' clubs, and clergy groups debated methods of water protection, and many of their members began to take an interest in the role that forests played in protecting drinking water. Lawyer and long-distance hiker Herbert Welsh rallied his wealthy neighbors to press for reforestation, and merchant groups campaigned for protecting forested watersheds to control floods and ensure navigable flows in the state's primary rivers.[30]

At the urging of urban residents and townspeople who feared for their water supplies, the legislature created the Pennsylvania Forestry Commission in 1893 and the Pennsylvania Water Supply Commission in 1905. The two commissions would eventually be merged into one state department, since both entities were primarily engaged with protecting both rivers and trees.[31] When the Forestry Commission was first formed, it was specifically charged with studying the watersheds of the state to determine how they might best be protected.[32] Four years later, when the commission was given authority and funds to begin purchasing land, the legislature specified that the purchased land "shall become part of a forestry reservation system, having in view the preservation of the water supply at the sources of the rivers of the State, and for the protection of the people of the Commonwealth and their property from destructive floods."[33]

When Joseph T. Rothrock was appointed the state's first forestry commissioner in 1893, he had left a career as a physician to pursue botany and forest work. His experience with the U.S. Geological Survey out west, followed by a decade of studying and lecturing on Pennsylvania forests at both the University of Pennsylvania and the Academy of Natural Sciences, had already convinced him that cities, trees, water, and human health were intimately connected. Medical school at the University of Pennsylvania had initially been a compromise. It had been the only course of study offered there that would allow him to study biology, but biology of the plant world had always been his passion. By the time the state legislature finally created the Forestry Commission, Rothrock had been agitating for such a body for almost a decade; the year before, he had persuaded the Academy of Natural Sciences to at least pay his expenses for the forest survey and preservation work that he had been doing on his own until the state could get its act together and pass the necessary laws.[34]

When the legislature created the commission, the politicians charged Rothrock with figuring out how to aggregate and manage state-owned forestlands and also how to look toward managing private lands, where acres of standing forests were already protecting the streams that fed the cities. There were two threats to these private forests, in Rothrock's analysis: overharvesting and fire. Overharvesting could be (and was) somewhat curtailed by changes in the tax laws that had previously favored cleared land over land in trees. Fire protection, though, was a thornier problem, involving issues of equity across the state. In his campaign to change the way firefighting was financed in Pennsylvania, Rothrock insisted not only on cities' dependence on their hinterlands, but also on urban residents' responsibility for distant woods.

Drawing explicitly on connections between cities and forests, Rothrock successfully lobbied the legislature to change the way Pennsylvania handled its problem of out-of-control fires in remote areas. He argued convincingly that it was not only unfair but reckless that the state expected individual counties to take responsibility for forest fire suppression, which put an expensive, difficult burden on the least populated portions of the state. "Nothing more inequitable appears on our statute books than the law as it now stands," Rothrock wrote in his 1896 report. "The benefits of continuous even water flow, guarding against freshets on the one hand and low water on the other, accrue to the entire community. The most potent factor in ensuring this desirable condition is the forest cover upon the headwaters of the streams." Forcing the least populous counties to pay to protect the forest cover on which the cities were so dependent simply could not continue. "It is no mere figure of speech to say it threatens the continued prosperity of the Commonwealth," he wrote.[35]

He was lobbying a receptive audience. A few years earlier, the Philadelphia Board of Trade had made many of the same arguments to the legislature, in support of the bill that ultimately created Rothrock's job. With a

1.6 Saw mill and log pond in Sheffield, Pennsylvania. This was once the largest mill in the state. United States Forest Service Region 9, photograph R9_211678. Courtesy of the Forest History Society.

prescient understanding of the connections between cities and their hinterlands, Philadelphia's industrialists beseeched their political representatives to safeguard their water and trees. "Along the treeless hillsides and water-sheds in our State the constant flow of water for our uses would likely be insufficient and public health and safety endangered," the board members wrote, arguing that they were "fully aware of the important relation that the timber land of the State bears to the question of its water supply alone, to say nothing of its lumbering industry."[36]

Protecting standing timber from fire and purchasing tracts of forested land would not be enough. The state needed more trees, Rothrock argued, on both public and private property. "Strip it of collateral ideas and the fact at the bottom of the whole question is—the State must have a due proportion of woodland. It is an absolute condition upon which not only our prosperity but the very protection of the surface of the State depends," he wrote. "The first inquiry following is this: How can it be most surely, speedily and economically produced, by the State itself directly owning and directing the machinery, or by the State making it possible for the citizen to do this?"[37] Rothrock came down strongly on the side of the state, in part because of the benefits that would accrue to the entire commonwealth, but also because of the nature of forests and trees: "the century required to mature a crop of trees is as nothing to [the state], but is disheartening to the individual."[38]

How people were thinking about trees during the final years of the nineteenth century was as important as what they were doing to protect them. As Rothrock observed, a tree has a history and a future that are out of pace with human time; a forest even more so. It was only in the face of an imagined timber famine that urban residents and state and municipal politicians began to understand their fates as connected to the much longer lives of forests and trees. Individual fortunes, the fortunes of the state, and the health of cities and the nation could all be seen as connected through trees.

In 1897, when the Forestry Commission received its directive to protect urban water supplies by purchasing abandoned land for state forests, the state owned no land, save for the plots beneath state-owned buildings.[39] The next year, Commissioner Rothrock began purchasing land at county tax sales.[40] As was the case throughout the Northeast, farmers had abandoned many thousands of acres of marginal land when railroads made agricultural products from the West more competitive. Farmers in the southeast and far western portions of the state thrived, benefiting from the rich soils, flat country, and proximate urban markets. The hilly, rocky land to the north, at the headwaters of the state's rivers, did not fare so well. Much of the land Rothrock was initially able to purchase was abandoned terrain in the northern half of the state, which had been seized by local counties after owners failed to pay their property taxes.[41]

Not all abandoned land had been left by failed farmers in search of a better living. In 1880 Pennsylvania had been the nation's leading lumber producer, and timber companies continued impressive harvests of white pine, hemlock, maple, birch, and beech from the state's forests well into the early twentieth century.[42] Pennsylvania's land ownership patterns and tax structures, however, had encouraged cut-and-run lumbering techniques.

Many timber companies did not own the land on which they harvested trees, but rather purchased stumpage rights from owners for limited periods of time. The companies, therefore, had little incentive to log conservatively. In addition, a property tax system devised with the goal of encouraging settlers to clear land for farming placed a heavy tax on standing timber, so timber companies and woodlot owners alike found it most profitable to cut and sell their trees as soon as possible and then abandon the land before county taxes came due. Because there was little market for cutover land in Pennsylvania, much of the plundered timber land reverted to the county, which in turn sold it to the Forestry Commission for slightly more than the overdue taxes. In 1898, the Forestry Commission made its first purchase: 17,010 acres of abandoned land at an average price of fifteen cents per acre.[43]

Within the next few years, as speculators learned of the commission's plans to build a state forest system, fewer lands were available at such bargain prices. Opportunists bought up likely lots from the counties, quickly cut and sold any standing timber, and then tried to sell the denuded land to the state. County commissioners themselves got in on the schemes, and by 1902 the Forestry Commission was paying an average of $2.32 an acre. This opportun-

ism was curbed in 1905—though by no means stopped—when the legislature passed a law requiring county commissioners to give the Forestry Commission first option on abandoned lands.[44]

At the same time, the state's iron companies were selling forestland that they had intensively logged for years. In the eighteenth and nineteenth centuries, iron factories were fueled by charcoal made from the state's hardwoods. There were 145 charcoal furnaces operating in Pennsylvania during the Civil War, with each furnace consuming over twenty thousand acres of trees annually. Because of their dependence on a source of charcoal close to their factory sites, iron manufacturers tended to own forestland and manage it more conservatively than lumber operators, who were much more mobile. Most iron companies owned many times more land than they required for their annual fuel supply, and they counted on the forests' regeneration to supply their factories through the years. Some of the iron company land had been harvested three or four times by the end of the nineteenth century. By the time Rothrock and the Forestry Commission were looking to purchase forestland for the state, the iron producers had begun to replace wood with coal to run their furnaces, and so were eager to sell their tracts.[45]

The success of forest building in Pennsylvania, though, is not merely a story of new scientific ideas, real estate, and opportunity. It is also a story of passion—the passion of people like Rothrock, spurring the legislature and two governors to action and tirelessly seeking out new lands to put into

1.7 White and red pine plantations of Pennsylvania's York Water Company, 1928. The water company began raising trees for reforesting its watersheds in 1913. Commonwealth of Pennsylvania Department of Forests and Waters report to the Minnesota Reforestation Commission, 1928 [typescript and mounted photographs], photograph 1. Courtesy of the Forest History Society.

1.8 A corner of the Greenwood Forest Tree Nursery in Huntingdon County, Pennsylvania, site of the largest seed extraction plant on the Pennsylvania State Forests. The text accompanying this photograph explains that "in 1927, 1,324 bushels of cones were cleaned, yielding 1,164 pounds of seed." Commonwealth of Pennsylvania Department of Forests and Waters report to the Minnesota Reforestation Commission, 1928 [typescript and mounted photographs], photograph 9. Courtesy of the Forest History Society.

1.9 Mira Dock posing with her walking stick in the Pennsylvania woods. Public Relations Photographs, RG-6 Records of the Department of Forests and Waters—Forest Officials, Pennsylvania State Archives.

woods. It is also the story of women like Mira Lloyd Dock, who mobilized people across Pennsylvania and the nation to recognize an urban value in hinterland trees.

Dock, like Rothrock, had come to forestry in a roundabout way. Decades after Rothrock had studied medicine at the University of Pennsylvania as a gateway to studying trees, Dock enrolled at the University of Michigan to study botany. In 1896, at the age of forty-three, she had already raised five children, her younger siblings. Their mother had died early, leaving a teenage

Mira to see to the family, and it wasn't until each of the others had been set on the path to adulthood that she was able to pursue her own interests and career. From Michigan, she went to Germany, where she could get the forestry education unavailable to her in the United States. Yet an education was no guarantee of an academic post, and Dock was unable to secure the laboratory position that she had hoped to find. So instead of becoming a scientist, she embarked on a career of public speaking.[46]

Mira Dock's popular talks on cities' need for trees drew explicitly on the urban middle and upper classes' new taste for both travel and expert knowledge. Through her lively lectures, which she punctuated with glass-lantern slides of both beautiful and devastated spaces, she worked tirelessly to convince her listeners that their economy, health, and future depended on the woods. Both urban homes and country retreats depended on trees, she argued, and her receptive audiences took her message to heart. She explained in detail that trees were Pennsylvania's most critical resource and that safeguarding the few that were left and replanting bare hills and fields were essential to protecting wood, water, and soil.[47]

Her devotion to trees and their future had less to do with a love of nature, she frequently told people, than with love of people. Her intense interest in forestry had arisen from seeing a colony of woodcutters thrown out of work after a forest fire. Since then, she told her audiences, she had learned how crucial forested lands were to protecting the health and viability of all communities—urban and rural—throughout the state. People and trees, in Dock's experience, depended on one another. And the trees needed help.[48]

Aesthetics and ideas of purity and wildness held a strong power over the American imagination, and it was left to speakers and advocates like Dock to bring the concerns together in a way that average citizens could grasp and engage with. As Dock worked with forest advocates who had been pushing for forest protection on the basis of aesthetics, purity, and intrinsic value, she encouraged them to take up the language and ideas of scientific conservationists.

The newly accepted scientific connections between forests and urban water supplies brought people who had previously given little thought to trees into the forest-activism fold. Pennsylvania cities had been struggling with water quality issues for years, and if trees could help, Pennsylvanians wanted more of them. Dock's status as a popular forest advocate in the state, and one who was bringing in female audiences often neglected by others, brought her to the attention of the governor as someone who could be crucial to the cause.

Just as the new state Forestry Commission began its large-scale purchases of forestlands, Dock joined its ranks. Once Governor William Stone appointed Dock as one of the commissioners because of her expert knowledge and her transfixing public-speaking style, she used the platform of the commission to continue her ongoing forestry education campaign. Just as Philadelphians continued to worry about development upstream on the Schuylkill, Dock and her fellow Harrisburg residents were worried about the Susquehanna. Dock had come to believe that a healthy urban environment, predicated in large part on pure drinking water, required control of land beyond the city's borders.[49]

In December 1900, when Dock gave a glass-lantern slide lecture to the Harrisburg Civic Club, she spoke on water and trees. J. Horace McFarland, a leading Harrisburg businessman and City Beautiful activist, reported that at her talk, "Hundreds of men realized for the first time that a beautiful riverbank was not the best place for a public dump and that a modern city owes to its inhabitants something more than taxation, police protection, typhoid-laden water, imperfect sewerage and partial fire-protection."[50] Dock's emphasis on the connections between forest preservation and urban health and beauty was one many audience members had never considered before.

Dock traveled extensively throughout the state on speaking engagements and Forestry Commission business. Just as she advocated for the protection of Harrisburg's watershed, she was concerned about the watersheds of Philadelphia and Pittsburgh, and spoke forcefully about the ramifications of logging for people downstream, pushing for an expanded role for both the state and the federal government in managing the watersheds of major rivers.[51]

Both her statewide and national tours prompted Dock to get more involved in the woods near her home—hiking, planting, digging in the dirt, and creating new forests near Harrisburg that had not existed before. Shortly after her Civic Club talk in Harrisburg, McFarland and other Harrisburg business leaders banded together to hire other experts for advice on addressing the city's dire need for water and trees. Water supply specialist James H. Fuertes of New York and park planner Warren H. Manning of Boston included among their recommendations a plan for a large park north of the city, turning to Dock to educate them on local conditions. Wetzel's Swamp had been one of her pet projects, and it became a focus for the new work of the city's outside experts.[52]

Wetzel's Swamp had once been marginal farmland, but by the time Fuertes and Manning surveyed it, it had long been "a resort for tramps" and a "burial ground for deceased domestic animals." With the clearing of the remaining ramshackle structures on the land, Manning argued, Harrisburg's citizens could secure for themselves "about five hundred acres of swamp and dry land, framed in with wooded bluffs on one side and a line of fine old willows along the canal on the other. . . . It is rare, indeed, that a city can secure a property having all the elements of a park landscape, its border-planting of fine trees, splendid individual specimens, and woodlands carpeted in spring with numerous wild flowers."[53]

Best of all, a dam on Paxton Creek within the park would help with flood control for the downstream city, while also creating a reservoir of clean, protected drinking water just upstream from the Susquehanna. The city didn't have enough money to purchase all of the land in what would become Wildwood Park right away, but the experts recommended purchasing several crucial parcels at once.[54]

Dock, McFarland, and their fellow park advocates worked hard to win city residents over to the plan. They gave slide talks, placed newspaper advertisements, arranged public gatherings, and pressured political candidates. They gathered enough support to secure a city property tax for park development, and by 1908 almost all of the recommended five hundred acres had been purchased, as well as an additional two hundred acres along the Susquehanna. At the same time, the city established its own tree nursery.[55]

The nursery, another of Dock's cherished projects, had the support of the new Harrisburg Park Commission, whose members included Horace

McFarland. "The Park Commission would be delighted to have the little pine forest you want to start for us, and I will say right now that the Commission will be more than willing," he wrote to Dock in September 1905. As he often did in his correspondence with Dock, McFarland joked about how their expertise was benefiting the city residents, sometimes in spite of themselves: "I will also say, privately, just in your ear, not to be mentioned, entre nous, that some of the members of our Commission do not know a pine from a pumpkin. . . . These people, however, give me almost a free hand, and the way in which I am meddling in most everything these days would make your hair stand on end if it was as short as mine!"[56] Thousands of trees from the nursery were planted along the riverbanks, and thousands more were planted at Wetzel's Swamp.[57] The twin concerns of aesthetics and water quality had led to the reforestation of the Harrisburg watershed.

The state's Forestry Commission established small nurseries on most of the state forests, and opened a large facility in Franklin County in 1903 and another in Clearfield County in 1911. At first, the nurseries were solely supplying the new state lands, but by 1910 they had begun providing trees at cost to anyone who wanted them. By 1923 almost thirty-five million seedlings had been planted in Pennsylvania, with more being planted each year. The number of trees itself is small—a thousand or more seedlings might be planted on a single acre—but the project was important: trees were available to anyone who wanted them, and people ordered them by the dozens and the hundreds. Pennsylvanians knew that they had a role in bringing trees back to their lands, and the nurseries fed that knowledge and created a need.[58]

Nurseries were only part of the story. Since the Forestry Commission made its first land purchases in 1897, the state had been slowly acquiring land to be set aside for trees. By 1904 the state had acquired more than a half million acres of forest reserve land, most of it land that had been abandoned by its owners. By 1914 the state controlled in excess of one million acres. At the end of the twentieth century, there were over two million acres of state forest reserves, and another half million acres of forests in state parks and game lands.[59]

By 1908 Mira Dock was advising other states and the federal government

1.10 Harvesting seed. This photograph is mounted on a blue piece of paper with the typed explanation: "First class trees, like prime beef cattle or Grade A potatoes, depend upon high grade parent stock. Young trees, from which seed is being collected here in Pennsylvania, are not usually as desirable as those of greater maturity which show rapid growth and good form." Forest History Society Image Collection Folder "Reforestation—Planting, Hand 3/3." Courtesy of the Forest History Society.

on how to emulate Pennsylvania's success in forest and watershed management, and she was corresponding with Philadelphia lawyer Herbert Welsh about forest protection in the Northeast. Pennsylvania, with its burgeoning urban populations dependent on watersheds that had been ravished by agriculture and the iron and lumber industries, had been an early leader in forest protection. As other states became interested in the science of forestry and in protecting their water and woods, they often turned to Pennsylvania's experts for advice, and the state's forest advocates, energized by their successes, preached the message of reforestation wherever they got the chance. In a 1908 letter to Thomas Will, the secretary of the American Forestry Association, Dock boasted about the "remarkable work" being done by Pennsylvania state agencies in protecting the resources of both the state and the nation. The only waters of the Potomac, the major river in the nation's capital, that were in any degree protected, she wrote, were "within the boundaries of Pennsylvania, where in fact they [were] triply protected by the State Forest, Water and Health Departments." The national organization, she argued, should learn from Pennsylvania's example and devote more space in its publication *Forestry and Irrigation* to the state's dramatic success.[60]

More than three million acres of new forests in Pennsylvania can be directly linked to efforts to secure drinking water for urban residents. In the twentieth century, most cities—both in Pennsylvania and elsewhere—added water treatment and filtration plants to their municipal supply systems, no longer depending on forests alone to protect the supply. Nevertheless, by the end of that century, more than a hundred municipalities in Pennsylvania were dependent on state forests for their drinking water supplies. At least two dozen cities and towns have reservoirs within state forest boundaries, and three times that many have reservoirs adjacent to state lands.[61]

Working together as forestry commissioners, Rothrock and Dock were focused on educating the public, state bureaucrats, city politicians, and industrialists on the vital links between cities, economies, and trees. In their campaigns for expanding and protecting Pennsylvania's forested lands, they each drew on their expertise and training in botany, forestry, and hydrology, as well as fledgling ideas about intricate connections within biological systems that decades later would be recognized as central tenets of ecology. Dock and Rothrock worked tirelessly to convince the public of the connections among potable water, navigable streams, clean air, urban beauty, health, and trees.[62] To win public support for their programs, they capitalized on the growing popular audiences for scientific knowledge while also drawing on aesthetic and romantic ideas about the value of trees. They spoke of grand beauty and intrinsic value in woods and drove their points home with forceful claims of scientific authority: a region without forests would be a region without water. Cities depended on trees to slake their thirst.

Urban residents continue to depend on forests, the seemingly natural landscapes that are in fact artifacts of the city. The reservoirs, woods, and urban spaces and the people who shaped all three are integral components of the region's ecological systems. The forests, with their dams and reservoirs and protected riverbanks, are not just bucolic picnic spots. Neither are they the result of benign neglect on the part of a newly urban population. The new forests in Pennsylvania, and elsewhere in the Northeast, are the result of attitudes, ideas, priorities, and laws that were developed and established at the end of the nineteenth century and the beginning of the twentieth. They have become indispensable parts of the landscape of the twenty-first-century urban Northeast, as constructed as the cities are themselves.[63] And the popular understandings of the physical workings and the health benefits of forests and rivers that were at the core of the policies and programs to protect and create woods got much of their start in Philadelphia, in Harrisburg, in Pittsburgh, and in smaller cities and towns across Pennsylvania.

Concerns about the purity and reliability of water supplies from rivers and streams had led Pennsylvanians to claim an interest in forest activities beyond their cities, and ultimately beyond their state borders. As they realized that activities anywhere within a watershed could have serious local ramifications, Pennsylvanians, along with New Yorkers and New Englanders, began to see a larger landscape as within their proper realm of influence and control.

Distant threats to water supplies led people throughout the Northeast to begin thinking regionally about their resources. Early proponents of New York's Adirondack Park, established in 1892, joined the campaign for protecting upstate lands because they were worried about water levels in the Hudson River. New York City businessmen, concerned that irregular flows in the river could impede their access to markets, saw forest protection as a way to stave off that threat. And in the early twentieth century, both Boston and New York City secured jurisdiction over upstate lands to protect their drinking water supplies, which led to dramatic reforestation in those regions. New Haven, Providence, and smaller cities throughout New England took measures to preserve and restore forests on their watershed lands.[64] Private groups, trade organizations, and individuals pressured municipal governments, state legislatures, and the national government to protect the banks of rivers and reservoirs with trees.

For Dock, Welsh, and many other Pennsylvanians, landscapes from Washington, D.C., to Maine suddenly seemed far closer to home. And after spending the winters campaigning for trees in Pennsylvania and spending the spring walking through the forests of New England, Philadelphia lawyer Herbert Welsh carried his campaign to save forests to the mountains of New Hampshire. In 1909, he and his fellow vacationers from the city saw new threats to the wooded lands surrounding their hinterland homes. The work he helped coordinate there would ultimately lead not only to a secure future for thousands of acres of forestland near his vacation home but also to the creation and protection of another half million acres of woodlands in Pennsylvania. The Allegheny National Forest was made possible by the people who found a way to make preserving the trees of the White Mountains a national priority.[65]

1.11   A selectively cut northern hardwood stand in Cherry Run, Pennsylvania, 1952.
American Forest Products Industries Photo. Forest History Society Image Collection Folder
"Reforestation—Natural, East and South 4/6." Courtesy of the Forest History Society.

CHAPTER TWO

New Hampshire Watersheds, Viewsheds, and Timber

A s August gave way to September in 1909 and Lake Sunapee vacationers were closing up their summer houses before returning to Boston, New York, Philadelphia, or Washington, D.C., Philadelphia lawyer Herbert Welsh noticed that loggers were cutting down trees on the mountain across the lake, destroying his view. Angry, he promptly rallied his neighbors behind an emergency campaign. The summer residents who shared Welsh's outrage at the clear-cuts were people of wealth and prestige: Clara Louise Hay, widow of the late Secretary of State John Hay; New York City physician John Quackenbos; Columbia University history professor William Dunning; and New Yorkers Annis and Carrie Covell, who owned Sunapee's prestigious Grandliden Hotel. As the weather began to turn, they were each on their way back to city lives, but not before safeguarding the primary amenity that made their lakeshore homes worth the long, seasonal trek: a feeling of wildness that separated them from the industry and mess of the city and that depended on a view of forests from their porches. They quickly raised eight thousand dollars to purchase the "butchered" land, which by the end of the year would become New Hampshire's first forest reserve.[1]

In many ways, this early twentieth-century maneuver by "outsiders" to

2.1 Lake Sunapee, viewed from Sunapee Mountain, New Hampshire, ca. 1900. Library of Congress, Prints & Photographs Division, Detroit Publishing Company Collection, LC-D4-11737.

2.2 The steamer *Armenia White* on Lake Sunapee, New Hampshire, ca. 1900. Library of Congress, Prints & Photographs Division, Detroit Publishing Company Collection, LC-D4-11742.

purchase, replant, and protect a forested hillside in order to maintain their summer playground is a microcosm of a campaign that was already under way in Washington, D.C. Philadelphians, New Yorkers, and Bostonians who summered in New Hampshire were among the most influential backers of the national legislation that made eastern national forests possible. After years of running up against both constitutional hurdles and timber industry opposition, Congress finally passed the Weeks Act in 1911, giving the federal government the right to purchase land in the service of protecting watersheds of navigable rivers that crossed state lines. Many of its backers cared more about viewsheds than watersheds—what they could see from their porch or from the hiking trail, rather than how trees would regulate stream flow for interstate commerce—but the interstate commerce clause of Article 1 of the U.S. Constitution provided the legal mechanism that the federal government required.

National forests in the West could be carved out of the abundant federally owned lands there, but the federal government owned no land in the East. No matter how good an idea it seemed to be, nothing in the constitution implied that the federal government had the power to buy land in order to create or protect a forest for its beauty. An argument could be made for protecting a forest for its function, and so water became central to protecting views. The Weeks Act accomplished on a national scale what the Lake Sunapee vacationers accomplished in their backyards. After 1911, the federal government began purchasing the land that would become the White Mountain National Forest in New Hampshire and Maine, the Green Mountain National Forest in Vermont, the Allegheny National Forest in Pennsylvania, and a myriad of parcels that became federally protected eastern forestland.

Scenery, hiking, property values, love of nature—all were key to the creation of both the state forest at Sunapee and the White Mountain National Forest farther north. Money and legal maneuvering were equally important. But the new forests in both places were not merely the projects of rich people protecting what they imagined to be pristine playgrounds, though that is the story most often told. The full history of the protection of New Hampshire woods is a more complicated one of local industrial interests, changing economies, innovations in transportation, and changing ideas about who

NEW HAMPSHIRE

White Mountain
National Forest

Mount Washington

Lake Winnipesaukee

Lake Sunapee

Mount Sunapee   ★ Concord

Manchester •

2.3   Important locations in New Hampshire. Map by Rachel Hope Allison.

should care about trees and why. The forests of Mount Sunapee and Craw-ford Notch (the first parcel of land purchased by the federal government in the White Mountains) gave visitors a sense of the wild, and they gave locals a sense of the future. The Sunapee summer people were able to purchase and protect the hillside that decorated the banks of their lake for the same reason the federal government was able to purchase 12 percent of the state for a forest reserve. New Hampshire residents—farmers, laborers, and business owners alike—also wanted and needed the trees.

New Hampshire, like Pennsylvania, seemed to be facing the disappearance of its woods in the nineteenth century, yet saw a resurgence of trees in the twentieth and twenty-first. In the mid-nineteenth century, only 50 percent of New Hampshire was forested; by the early years of the twenty-first century, that figure was 86 percent. As elsewhere in the region, the forests

NEW HAMPSHIRE

Forest Cover

- 1 to 25%
- 26 to 50%
- 51 to 75%
- 76 to 100%

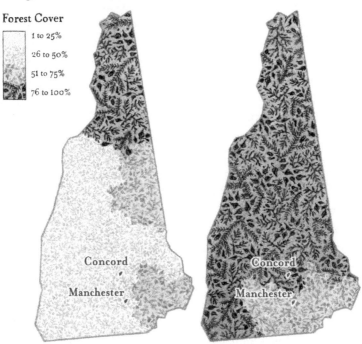

Concord

Manchester

Early Twentieth Century

Concord

Manchester

Late Twentieth Century

2.4 The increase in forest cover in New Hampshire during the twentieth century. Map by Rachel Hope Allison.

began their rebirth after farmers began to keep fewer fields clear for crops in the face of competition from newly accessible, more productive farmland to the west.

Yet struggling New Hampshire farmers did not merely move away and leave their land to trees. Nor did they simply lay down their plows and begin leading hikes through scraggly fields and cutover woods that would magically become today's treasured and seemingly pristine White Mountain National Forest. Instead, they planted trees. They courted tourists. They changed tax policies. They found new ways to make a living from their land. To understand how Crawford Notch, Mount Sunapee, the rustic huts of the Appalachian Trail, and the forests that blanket them became the most famous and economically crucial features of twenty-first-century New Hampshire is to understand that distant cities, local farmers, and New Hampshire business owners needed those trees, worked hard to bring them back, and have protected them since their return.[2]

Trees could have come back to New Hampshire of their own accord, but they often had help. Spruce and pine, in particular, were planted, protected, and encouraged, as former farmers and newly trained foresters nurtured and managed new forests for both summer and year-round residents of the state. The trees were a crop of useful wood: they were bobbins, coffins, and railroad ties; they were boxes and bins and tools; and they were boards for building new homes, new inns, new hotels. The trees were beauty: they created the atmosphere and sense of timeless, undisturbed nature along mountain hikes and railroad rides. And as in Pennsylvania, they were tools: forests held water in mountain soils to prevent floods in spring and droughts in summer.

Foresters and activists in the two states traded ideas and shared expertise, and New Hampshire forest activists learned from Pennsylvania's early examples. But in the nineteenth century, Pennsylvania was a far more urban state than its northern cousins, which meant that Pennsylvania's arguments for protecting water and trees together were most often tied to the need for clean and reliable drinking water for growing city populations. In New Hampshire, the impulses also flowed from the city, but in the form of concern over summer scenery and—just as important for getting the legislation passed—

worries about reliable water supplies for mills. In both places, the idea of a watershed was a new and dramatically influential one, providing remarkable rhetorical power for the forest protection fight.

In American forestry and land-use planning, a watershed has long been understood as the area draining into a particular river, stream, ocean outlet, or lake. Watersheds are contained in watersheds: a creek's watershed may be relatively small, but when it drains into a river, it becomes part of the river's watershed, along with those of all the other tributaries that join the river on its journey downstream. Watersheds tie landscapes together, and in the early twentieth century, the idea of a watershed allowed travelers to understand how damage to a seemingly remote mountain hillside might have consequences for water supplies at home. Just as trains were collapsing time and space for people a century ago, watersheds were tying distant places together into single landscapes with shared ecologies.

Though the word would have made people laugh at the time, modern land-use planners use an analogous term to describe what Welsh and his neighbors wanted to protect: their viewshed. Just as the ecology of Lake Sunapee is shaped by every drop of water that flows down hills and streams to the lake, the experience of a summer escape to nature is shaped by everything that flows to a vacationer's sight line. In a viewshed, as in a watershed, seemingly unconnected landscapes become recognizably intertwined. The word is awkward and anachronistic but conceptually useful in understanding what it was and is that so motivates many conservationists: protecting all that the eye can take in.

Yet even the concept of a watershed is more useful than it is precise. Its original definition meant something far different than its popular understanding. The concept as it was used by New Hampshire and Pennsylvania forest activists and enshrined in federal legislation by the Weeks Act in 1911 was peculiarly American, based on a misunderstanding of a term from German land management, the *Wasserscheide*. A *Wasserscheide* as nineteenth-century German foresters defined it was not the entire basin that drained into a body of water; it was the break between two such basins. The watershed was the dividing line: a raindrop falling to the west of such a line might drain to the Mississippi, for example, while a raindrop falling to the east would drain to the Atlantic Ocean. A watershed did not unify; it defined a break.

This is the only definition that makes sense in our metaphorical use of the word. A "watershed moment" is one that marks a dramatic break from the past; everything that follows is different from before. For northeastern American forests, both senses are correct. When popular ideas of unified landscapes allowed tourists, politicians, mill owners, lumbermen, city residents, and rural famers to understand their fates as tied together by water and forests, history shifted for the region's trees. What had seemed to be a personal concern or at most a local issue became a matter of national import: forested land that fed and protected rivers flowing though the region's many states was under threat.

The details, personalities, and individual choices at Sunapee help illuminate what was happening on the national stage. This very local story was a national one, tied both to cities farther south and to mountains to the north. Cities, vacation spots, and distant hinterlands were newly intertwined—by both technology and imagination—and that meant a new future for trees. Those connections would later be lost and the forests thereby imperiled, but for the moment new ideas and new tools meant new trees.

In 1909, when the campaign to save the Sunapee forest began, the summer people, the loggers, and even the trees themselves were newcomers to the area. The land that so interested Herbert Welsh and his neighbors had been farmed by the Johnson family since the 1820s and had long been field, not forest. But when the railroad reached the base of Sunapee Mountain in 1849, it brought with it competition from distant markets, and Nathan Johnson struggled to keep his farm profitable. To supplement income from his sheep and cows and his crops of potatoes and corn, Nathan chose to capitalize on the other effect of the train's arrival: tourists needed places to stay. In the late 1860s, he built a fashionable resort hotel on his land that could accommodate more than a hundred guests. The land nearest the hotel was no longer active farmland and began to return to trees.[3]

Other farmers across New Hampshire made similar decisions. Before the Civil War, farmers had been able to support themselves by supplying nearby markets with grain and meat. Even though much of the New Hampshire soil outside of the Connecticut and Merrimack river valleys is poor and rocky, high local demand made the business viable, even with low yields. With the coming of the railroads in the 1840s and 1850s, however, and the accompanying competition from western farmers, who had more productive land, New Hampshire farmers needed new strategies to survive.[4]

Some farmers turned to more perishable products, such as milk and produce, for which proximity to markets remained an advantage.[5] Others, like Johnson, looked to the fledgling tourist industry to supplement a declining income from crops. Still others turned to wage labor in the state's booming mill towns or left for Ohio, Indiana, or Illinois.[6] In 1850 two-thirds of the state had been classified as improved farmland; by 1900 only one-third was still "improved." The abandoned fields often returned to woods.[7]

Along with the arrival of tourists and trains, textile mills were also changing the shape of New Hampshire. After 1814, a series of locks and canals made it possible to travel the Merrimack River all the way from Concord, New Hampshire, to Boston. A few years later, the Boston Associates, fresh from their successful textile mill venture in Waltham, Massachusetts, explored the newly accessible Merrimack for mill sites. At Lowell, Massachusetts, they constructed the first of the large textile mills in the valley. By the mid-nineteenth century, over forty Waltham-Lowell style mills operated along the Merrimack in Massachusetts and New Hampshire.[8] Similarly, the Saco, Androscoggin, and Connecticut rivers provided power to dozens of textile mills throughout the state. All four rivers found their headwaters in the White Mountains, making the mills dependent on forested watersheds.[9]

Meanwhile, the railroads barreled up the steep, forested hillsides of the White Mountains. Much of the northern part of the state had been relatively inaccessible until the trains arrived, and the land remained under state ownership. The railroads, however, brought the land within reach, and in 1867 New Hampshire's governor Walter Harriman sold the last of New Hampshire's public domain to timber companies eager to bring the mountains' trees to market. The railroad itself was a major source of timber consumption, utilizing thousands of cords a year for fuel and ties. At the same time, though, the

2.5   Mill pond and bobbin mill in Whitefield, New Hampshire. United States Forest Service Region 9, photograph R9_ 212009. Courtesy of the Forest History Society.

trains were bringing tourists to the Whites, and the tourists loved the trees. A conflict over the future of forests in northern New Hampshire took root.[10]

As early as the 1880s, the legislature identified the future of New Hampshire forests as critical for the state's economy, as a resource for both the timber and the tourist industries. In 1881, amid growing national concern about the future of the nation's forest resources, and in the same year that the U.S. Congress first established a division of forestry within the Department of Agriculture, New Hampshire appointed its first forestry commission. Reappointed in 1883, it became a permanent part of New Hampshire state government in 1893.[11] The Forestry Commission, the Board of Agriculture, and the Tourism Commission were all concerned with the future of New Hampshire's forests. Back at Sunapee, the Johnson family's changing economic strategies illustrate the connections between the three concerns.

By the late nineteenth century on Mount Sunapee, overlooking the lake where moneyed Philadelphians, New Yorkers, and Bostonians summered, the Johnson family must have felt itself caught and somewhat jangled by the new technologies that were transforming New Hampshire. Their changing economic strategies parallel ways that many area families changed their lives and habits to make ends meet in what seemed like a new world.

By building their large hotel, the Johnson family made their farm into a tourist destination as well as a place of agricultural production.[12] In the years immediately after Johnson's Mountain House was built, guests were met at the Newbury Railroad Station at the base of Mount Sunapee, and brought up the steep dirt road to the hotel by horse and wagon. Once they arrived, they were treated to hearty meals, solicitous service and luxurious accommodations. But barely a decade after the grand resort opened its doors, it—like so many other grand wood structures of the day—was destroyed by fire.

The Johnsons did not rebuild, but they continued to serve seasonal tourists by taking in boarders at their large farmhouse, which could accommodate twelve guests at a time. Finally, in 1906, with Nathan's health failing and his son Ralph working at a hotel near Lake Sunapee and quarrying granite for the booming summer cottage and hotel industry, the Johnsons moved off the mountain. By that time, they had long been making more money from tour-

From This—
Broadway, New York City.

Photo. by Underwood & Underwood, N. Y.

To This.
The Road to River Hill, Penacook.

2.6 A 1913 New Hampshire advertising booklet emphasized just how easy it was to move from the middle of the city to country life. How pleasant to move "From This—" *New Hampshire Farms for Summer Homes* (Concord: State Board of Agriculture, 1913), 8. Courtesy of the University of New Hampshire Milne Special Collections and Archives.

2.7 "To This." *New Hampshire Farms for Summer Homes* (Concord: State Board of Agriculture, 1913), 9. Courtesy of the University of New Hampshire Milne Special Collections and Archives.

ists than from agriculture, and much of their former crop and pastureland had already reverted to woods.[13]

Although the Johnsons still owned their farm and continued to grow hay and potatoes for the next couple of decades, the state of New Hampshire now officially classified their farm as abandoned: the owners had moved away, and the land was no longer under intense cultivation. And this, for the state, was a problem. Overgrown fields, falling-down farm buildings, and collapsing fences were not what local politicians wanted wealthy New Yorkers, Bostonians, and Philadelphians to see when they visited New Hampshire.

As the nineteenth century drew to a close, the legislature charged the Board of Agriculture with addressing the problem of unsightly and unproductive farms.[14] In 1889, the board began publishing a catalogue of New Hampshire's abandoned farms, marketing such parcels as perfect, inexpensive summer places for city residents in search of country retreats. "New Hampshire Farms for Summer Homes" proved a great success.[15]

In its first year of surveying abandoned farms, the Board of Agriculture identified 1,342 farms with buildings suitable for dwelling, included them in the "Summer Homes" publication, and mailed six thousand copies around the country. Inquiries came from as far away as North Dakota, California, and London, and three hundred had been sold by the end of the first year's campaign. "A large number of these farms have become occupied by city people to whom a home in the country has been a fond anticipation for many years," Commissioner of Agriculture N. J. Bachelder explained, "and it is needless to say that they will find in a New Hampshire farm all the opportunities for gratifying any worthy desire in establishing a home for comfort, health, or pleasure. They come, not to make money but to spend it, and fortunate indeed will it be for the State when the unsold abandoned farms are utilized by this class of people." The Board of Agriculture was courting tourists and their dollars.[16]

From the board's perspective, getting tourists to purchase land had three major benefits. First, as newcomers improved their country estates, they would add to property tax coffers. Second, the farms would remain out of agricultural production, reducing competition among the remaining farmers.

Third, the summer people would need to buy milk, eggs, and fresh fruits and vegetables and thus would be a new market for those continuing to farm. Commissioner Bachelder emphasized this last point: "Although the summer boarding business cannot be strictly claimed as a farm industry, yet it is one of the ways in which our New Hampshire farms are being benefited. From the best statistics at our command, there have been left in the State by summer tourists during the year more than $5,000,000. A large portion of this has been left with the farmers." By summering on former farms, city tourists could preserve the profitability of those farms that remained.[17]

In New Hampshire, when a farmer began to devote less time to keeping his fields and pastures clear, trees quickly encroached on the land. Spruce and fir took over the old fields in the coolest regions, while white pine and hemlock moved in at lower elevations.[18] By the time the Johnsons moved off the mountain, much of their pastureland had been reclaimed by spruce trees, mixed with the beech, birch, and maple common to local newly reforested land that had formerly been grazed and trampled by cows. Former cropland, where soils were less compacted and young sprouts were less likely to have been munched away, saw a different mixture of trees. There, amid weeds and vestiges of cultivated plants, the hardwoods—liking sun—crowded out the young spruce that needed shade in order to take proper root. Land that had been sheared for timber but not cleared for pasture or field came back in yet different ways, more likely to be naturally reseeded by the recently harvested trees, for example, depending on how the cuts had been carried out. Throughout the state, new timber growth on all of these lands was an attractive commodity for local mills, which had begun to turn to out-of-state sources for almost half of the raw materials required for the rakes, crutches, boxes, barrels, coffins, furniture, and farm tools that they produced, as well as for the lumber to supply the booming building trades.[19]

New Hampshire farmers, then, had conflicting interests when it came to their woodlots. On the one hand, the tourists were much more interested in seeing trees than timber operations, and maintaining the scenery for their enjoyment was important. On the other, farmers could make money by selling trees. Often, state tax policy made the decision clearer: not only did farmers make money from selling timber, but clearing land reduced property taxes as well. In New Hampshire, as in much of the Northeast, standing timber was taxed on its full value each year—the sooner it was cut, the less tax a farmer had to pay. This policy had made sense when the state's goal had been to encourage agriculture, but it did not fit with new interests in preserving the forested landscape for scenery and sustainable forestry.

Despite repeated attempts by farmers and conservationists, incentives to clear-cut land were not entirely weeded out of the tax code until 1942. Incremental changes made a big difference, though, and are part of why twenty-first-century New Hampshire is almost entirely in woods, mainly in private hands. Over a million acres of the state, about 20 percent of the land, is in publicly owned state, federal, and municipal forests today, which is remarkable in a state that had no public forests and few trees a century ago. But the state is over 80 percent forested, which means that the vast majority of New Hampshire's woods are privately owned. Some of that is corporate timberland, but much of it is in small woodlots—some planted, some merely encouraged, nearly all set aside and nurtured during the first years of the twentieth century when incremental changes in taxation meant that letting trees grow could cost a farmer less money than cutting them down, and when planting a field in pine or spruce could be a revenue-positive endeavor.[20]

Beginning in 1903, any New Hampshire landowner who held fewer than five hundred acres could get a property tax rebate of up to 80 percent for any land that had been planted with at least three hundred trees per acre. The rebate could be claimed every year for thirty-five years, as long as the young trees continued to grow and the stand was well cared for.[21] The law was hard to take advantage of, though, and those who wanted to promote reforestation in the state kept pushing for more change. Among those working for tax law revision was J. B. Harrison, one of New Hampshire's early forest commissioners and a frequent summer visitor at Lake Sunapee, where he was part of the summer social circle of long-distance hiker Herbert Welsh. Welsh and Harrison knew each other not just from summer months spent in each other's company, but also from working together on forest conservation campaigns in New York and Pennsylvania. New Hampshire was also Harrison's permanent home, and by the last decade of the nineteenth century he felt himself to be called by God to devote himself full time to forest conservation in that state.[22]

Harrison was literally worried sick over the condition of New Hampshire's forests.[23] His position as a forest commissioner was unpaid and the fledgling state body had no real power. His colleagues on the commission had little time or energy to devote to the forest project beyond the commission's mandated goal of creating a report on the state of New Hampshire forests. While Harrison understood their limits, he was nonetheless frustrated, because for him, forest protection was more a calling than either a pastime or business concern.[24] "The other members of the Commission are excellent men, in full sympathy, but busy men of affairs, necessarily keeping strictly to the official duties of our Commission," Harrison told his good friend Welsh. But for Harrison, the forestry crisis was "entirely personal."[25] He fretted so much about trees that he sank into a depression. The only way out that he could see was to make the forests his life's work.

Harrison and his wife were struggling financially, and Mrs. Harrison was seriously ill. Even so, J. B. was unable to sit idly by and watch the landscape being destroyed. He felt compelled to launch a public speaking and pamphleteering campaign to protect New Hampshire's woods at his own expense. He wrote to Welsh: "I was so burdened by what I saw of 'the slow approach of doom' for our state, and the sense of my own helplessness, that I was becoming ill, and Mrs. Harrison said I would better begin, anyway, whether we could live or not."[26] The moral imperative to save the trees simply overwhelmed all else.

Harrison explained his concerns: First, he worried about the future timber supply of the state. How could the people of New Hampshire survive without trees for mills, lumber for homes, wood to burn for heat? Second, he worried about the effect of deforestation on the flow of rivers, which could affect the reliability of water power along the Merrimack and Connecticut rivers. Losing the forests could mean losing water, which would mean no power and lost jobs. Third, he worried about what he called "the scenery interest." Forests were beautiful, and beauty brought people to New Hampshire.[27] All three

2.8 A view of returning trees along the Mount Washington Carriage Road, at Tuckerman's Ravine in New Hampshire's White Mountains, ca. 1861. Photograph by John P. Soule, 1828-1904 [detail]. P.9022.13. Courtesy of the Library Company of Philadelphia.

concerns, he believed, were central to the economic future of the state and were evidence that God intended New Hampshire to be covered in woods.

Harrison's concerns—if not his missionary zeal and sense of divine duty—were echoed by the official mission of the Forestry Commission, the letterhead of which stated its goal: "To promote rational methods of treatment of the mountain forests, water sources and scenery of New Hampshire."[28] Harrison spent endless hours pursuing that goal with whatever strategies he could muster. He lobbied the state's industrialists, trade organizations, and chambers of commerce, because he knew he needed their support to be successful in slowing the timber harvest. He published fliers and pamphlets, which he distributed in New Hampshire and neighboring states. He traveled around the region talking to civic organizations, government officials, mill owners, and lumbermen. And he spoke to newspaper reporters throughout the Northeast, drumming up far-ranging support for the conservation efforts he believed to be so critical to New Hampshire's future.[29]

Harrison's pragmatic approach, publicly emphasizing resource protection, combined with his sense of a spiritual and aesthetic imperative, carried the seeds of the strategy that would bring not only local land management and taxation changes that protected forests but also the passing of the Weeks Act to create the White Mountain National Forest. Harrison's heart was with the sylvan vistas, mountain cabins, and hiking trails, and he found allies among people who had no particular love for timber companies or textile mills. "It is all one great fight for the kingdom of God," he wrote to Welsh, "under the Great Leader and Captain, into whose service we are, all of us, born."[30] And it was the destruction of the kingdom of God that kept him up at night. When he sought financial support for his forestry campaigns, he turned not to the mill owners or workers, but to the summer residents of the state, who shared his Romantic love of trees.[31]

It was the combination of romance and pragmatism that brought forest preservation to the state. Two late nineteenth-century floods convinced farmers, mill owners, and mill workers that they shared an interest in reforestation with those who were promoting tourism. Harrison, Welsh, and their peers may have been inspired by a vision of pristine nature, but their success

2.9 The Willey House, Crawford Notch, in New Hampshire's White Mountains. The inn, which was established in 1825, was destroyed by fire in 1899. In *Franconia Notch and the Women Who Saved It* (Durham: University of New Hampshire Press, 2007), Kimberly A. Jarvis tells the story of the Willey family's demise in an 1826 landslide that both spared the house and created a tourist-courting legend of drama and tragedy (see pages 21-24). Glass stereographs-Langenheim-P-2006-33-15 [detail]. Courtesy of the Library Company of Philadelphia.

in securing protection for New Hampshire trees depended on the working landscape. Floodwaters convinced many of what pamphlets could not: the state, and the nation, and in particular the nation's cities needed the trees.

April 1895 brought a disastrous flood to the Merrimack and Connecticut river valleys, with the highest waters in memory. The *Concord Monitor* reported: "When on Easter Sunday, 1895, the Merrimack had risen to a point higher than at any time within the memory of any but the oldest inhabitants, and Concord feared for the safety of her dam at Sewall's Falls, and her bridges, it was confidently asserted that not another such flood would be seen for a quarter century." Eleven months later, the floodwaters hit again. The Amoskeag Mill of Manchester had scarcely recovered from the damage of the first flood when water hit again, this time higher and swifter than the year before. The flood of March 1896 dwarfed that of 1895 and caused panic. "It had never occurred to us that there was any likelihood of this city experiencing a worse flood than that of a year ago," marveled H. F. Straw of the Amoskeag Company. "We were wholly without anticipation of any such unprecedented freshet as this."[32]

Portions of the Amoskeag Mill remained closed for months, leaving many of the mill's 7,200 employees out of work for the spring.[33] Initial estimates of the cost to the city were close to a million dollars. Estimates of similarly catastrophic damage were reported at mill towns all along the Merrimack and the Connecticut. Mills were closed, and people were facing long periods of unemployment in Maine, New Hampshire, Vermont, and Massachusetts.[34]

Two major floods in such close succession panicked many people in the region. Had the lumbering in the rivers' headwaters in the White Mountains changed the hydrology of the landscape so radically that destructive spring freshets would be an annual occurrence? Would they be worse every year, as trees continued to be stripped from the mountainsides? Many were convinced that the answer to those questions was yes.[35]

The *Manchester Union* found such arguments to be widespread enough to warrant rebuttal in an editorial titled "The Lesson of It," just four days after the peak of the flood: "Several of the Massachusetts papers are begging the question in endeavoring to make a striking argument for the protection of forests out of the recent costly freshet. Under the same conditions it is scarcely probable that the flood would have been any smaller or the damage any less had there not been a tree felled in the State for the past quarter of a century."[36] Simply put, the editorial argued, there was too much rain in too short a time, and all the trees in the world could not have held the water in the soil. Nevertheless, the *Union* agreed that forest practices were problematic and that they could contribute to floods in the future: "It is still a disputed question whether the havoc among the New Hampshire forests has yet been carried far or fast enough to add to the danger of freshets under any circumstances." But if current practices continued, it could become a worry.[37]

T. Jefferson Coolidge, treasurer of the Amoskeag Company, was worried already. In his 1896 annual report, he warned that logging on the Merrimack's watershed was threatening the operation of the mill, the security of jobs, and profits.[38] He was raising an alarm that the *New York Times* had been sounding for years. In the early 1890s, the *Times* had a relatively small circulation of about ten thousand readers, most of them businessmen in the cities of the Northeast. The paper had warned them about the folly of heavy lumbering. All the towns and cities along the Merrimack were suffering at the hands of the logging industry, the paper reported, and the future of both the mills and the fledgling tourist industry were in jeopardy. "The business interests of the whole of New Hampshire are at stake in this matter."[39] And the railroads, "with a stupidity that is amazing in their managers," the *Times* reported, "are among the chief promoters of this forest devastation."[40] Their stupidity, according to the *Times*, lay in not recognizing their own business interests in safeguarding the long-term future of the mills, the cities, and the tourist industry.

The controversy over the future of the state's forests cannot be simplistically characterized as a struggle between tourists and loggers, or outsiders and locals, or nature lovers and businessmen. At the turn of the century in New Hampshire, there were conflicts among businesses, among groups of workers, and among individual landowners over the future of the trees. The floods, in particular, convinced many of those people that they had a common interest in slowing, if not stopping, the logging in the mountains.

2.10   Workers standing between the Amoskeag Cotton Houses (*left*) and Gingham Mill
(*right*), ca. 1880. Photograph AMC g0269, Amoskeag Manufacturing Company Glass Negative
Collection. Courtesy of the Manchester (N.H.) Historic Association.

Pamphleteering, editorializing, and speechmaking on behalf of the forests increased apace.[41]

In 1901, what had been a loose confederation of people with sometimes contradictory interests in the future of New Hampshire's forests formed a formal organization, the Society for the Protection of New Hampshire's Forests. Among the first members were former governor Frank W. Rollins, Ellen M. Mason of the New Hampshire Federation of Women's Clubs, and Sunapee resident and New York physician John D. Quackenbos. Membership expanded quickly and drew support from wealthy summer people, from farmers who resented the control the timber companies held over upstate lands, from mill owners and manufacturers' trade organizations, and from timber companies and lumber businesses themselves.[42]

The society proposed several strategies to the legislature in Concord for protecting the forest cover of the watersheds of the state's rivers. Bills regulating the diameter of trees to be cut were thwarted, and a bill mandating management rules was thought to be too complicated to draft, given the variety of forest conditions. Legislators believed that there was not enough of a tax base for the state to raise the funds to purchase the White Mountains, especially in the poor hill towns from which the forest had already been cut for lumber. Further taxation for forest purposes found particular resistance in those counties. The members of the Society for the Protection of New Hampshire Forests were frustrated. They began to look to the federal government for help.[43]

The first bills proposing the purchase of eastern lands for national forests were introduced in Congress in 1899. "In those early days," remembered Philip Ayres, the first forester hired by the Society for the Protection of New Hampshire Forests, "the proposition looked to many like a crazy one."[44] The would-be forest protectors had to find some justification for federal purchase of eastern forestlands, and watershed protection was where they pinned their hopes. Ayres explained that "the interstate character of the White Mountains is sufficiently established by the fact that the waters flowing from them—the Androscoggin, the Saco, the Merrimack and the Connecticut rivers—supply power to more factories than any other waters in the country, and their even flow is of vast importance, and the mountains are visited already by people from every state in the Union for rest and recreation of a kind found in few other places."[45] Especially since the 1895 and 1896 floods, watershed protection in New Hampshire was a pressing and widely shared concern.[46]

Nevertheless, the aesthetic concerns of powerful people who vacationed in New Hampshire certainly helped the cause to gain momentum. "The plan for a national reservation has the emphatic endorsement of President Roosevelt, Secretary Hay, and the senators and representatives from New Hampshire, and prominent citizens in all parts of New England are giving active support," reported Philip Ayres in 1903.[47] Hay, as well as many of the other "prominent citizens" behind the campaign, had an interest in the plan beyond its importance to interstate commerce. They had summer homes in New Hampshire and wanted to protect the forested landscape they had come to associate with their chosen vacation spots.

The first proposals for an eastern national forest focused solely on the southern Appalachians, and initially the nation's forester, Gifford Pinchot, was vehemently against the inclusion of the White Mountains in the plan because he was afraid that broadening the campaign would jeopardize his effort to create a southeastern national forest. But the chaplain of the Senate was one of the founding members of the Society for the Protection of New Hampshire Forests, and he convinced Pinchot to relent. In 1905, Dr. Edward Everett Hale, who was ill at the time, testified at the First American Forest Conference in Washington, D.C.

Hale was a big man, and three friends had to help him up onto the platform to speak. Despite, or perhaps in part because of his illness, his oratory made quite an impression. Philip Ayres reported that after hearing Hale's speech, Pennsylvania's state forester J. T. Rothrock leaned over to Pinchot and said, "Now, Gifford, your bill for a National Forest in the Southern Mountains has been tried out in Congress and failed. It always will fail until you get those Yankees behind it. You have got to have those New England votes and you might just as well agree to a National Forest in the White Mountains."[48] The year 1905 was also when Congress finally put the nation's forest reserves under Pinchot's direct control. Since 1898, he had been chief of the Department of Agriculture's Division of Forestry, but the forests themselves had been officially the purview of the Department of the Interior. In 1905, after years of prodding from Pinchot, Congress transferred control of the forests to the Department of Agriculture's new United States Forest Service, and Pinchot was named its first head. After Hale's speech, the first chief forester of the U.S. Forest Service saw his opportunity for yet broader influence and support, and the White Mountains finally had an advocate in Pinchot.[49]

It was as the Sunapee summer people campaigned to save the distant White Mountains that the forested landscape closer to their summer doorsteps came under threat. After the Johnsons moved off Mt. Sunapee in 1906 and began working in town, they sold portions of their land to the Emerson Company, a paper company interested in the spruce trees growing on the mountain. There were also large tracts of hardwoods on the land that Emerson purchased, for which the company had no use. The Draper Company purchased the standing hardwood from the Emerson Company, and used that timber to supply its local bobbin mill, which in turn supplied urban textile mills. George Draper arranged with the Johnson family for his loggers to stay in the family's old house on the portion of the property that the Johnsons still owned, and the Draper employees began clearing the mountainside of trees. The Johnson family house had gone from being a farmhouse to a summer inn to a loggers' camp in less than half a century, as the land on which it was located continued to be a source of income. The summer people, however, were displeased by this latest turn of events. They had become accustomed to the forested hillside.[50]

The summer people had one big problem when they set out to halt the mountain logging. They did not know the first thing about the land or the local community. They did not know who owned which parcels or who was doing the logging. They did not know how much the land was worth or the dollar value of the trees. And Herbert Welsh, William Dunning, Richard Colgate, and their neighbors had to get back to their city jobs. So they turned in two directions for help: first to Philip Ayres, the forester for the Society for the Protection of New Hampshire Forests, and then to a local farmer, Archie Gove.[51]

Ayres, who had been a writer and a teacher before becoming a professional forester, was by class and education almost a peer of the summer people. He differed from them, though, in two primary ways: although a native of Iowa, he had chosen to make New Hampshire his permanent home, and he was interested not only in the aesthetic charms of the forests but also in their economic value as timber.[52] He was a practical businessman, and it was often his job to negotiate the many competing interests in the Lake Sunapee woods. Lake Sunapee summer people were among the most active and preservation-minded members of the Forest Society, but the owner of the Draper Company and the regional superintendent of the Emerson Company were also members. Some were interested in reforestation because they were worried about the timber supply; others were worried about the scenery. Ayres did his best to define a common ground.[53]

Even Philip Ayres turned to Archie Gove for local expertise and logistical support. Gove owned his own farm, not far from the Draper logging operations. When the summer people were negotiating which parcels to purchase, Gove took them on tours of the land and served them lunch at his house afterward. At times, his family's farmhouse served as an inn for the city travelers, coming north from Boston, New York, or Philadelphia for a quick meeting or an investigative trip when their summer houses were closed for the season.

After the summer people secured the purchase of the 653 acres of land most visible from their lake homes, they put Gove in charge of replanting the parcel and, in later years, harvesting the growing timber. Although the summer people were adamant about preserving their view, Ayres and Gove had convinced them that there were biological, economic, and aesthetic benefits to judicious logging. Most importantly, there were strategic benefits. By acceding to a certain amount of managed forestry on the land, the summer people were able to secure the protected views with which they were most concerned.[54]

Ayres and Gove explained to Welsh and his neighbors that they had an ally in George Draper, owner of the Draper Company, if they were willing to negotiate with him. Draper had been frustrated by the terms of his contract with the Emerson Company, which had required him to remove all of the hardwoods from the Emerson land within eight years. He preferred to manage the timber more conservatively, thereby ensuring a long-term supply of hardwood for his bobbin mill. Draper agreed to sell the mountain land he owned to the Society for the Protection of New Hampshire Forests, if the society would grant him conservative harvesting rights on both that land and any land the society purchased from the Emerson Company. Eventually, at the urging of both Ayres and Gove, the society members agreed, and the Mount Sunapee Forest Reservation was secured.[55]

For the summer residents, the forest preservation campaign had been about preserving an aesthetic ideal; for George Draper, it had been about securing a dependable resource supply for the Newport bobbin mill; for Philip Ayres, it had been about the proper development of both timber supplies and forested vistas; for Archie Gove, as for Nathan and Ralph Johnson, it had been about preserving his farm and continuing to make a good living in a changing regional economy. Urban and rural interests together with industrial and recreational concerns found common ground in a need for trees.

Similarly diverse interests were behind the founding of the White Mountain National Forest. The Weeks Act, which finally authorized the federal purchase of forestlands in the East on the watersheds of navigable rivers, was passed in 1911, just as the Sunapee summer people were finalizing the purchase of their forested view. Eastern forest advocates had finally convinced the U.S. Congress that the region's river basins had to be reforested to protect urban and industrial water supplies. The role of the federal government was crucial, because the rivers and watersheds crossed state boundaries; Boston had to be protected in New Hampshire, New Hampshire in Maine, and Pennsylvania in New Jersey and New York.

The first big Weeks Act purchases were in the White Mountains in New Hampshire, the Alleghenies in Pennsylvania, and the Southern Appalachians in North Carolina. Although land purchases were begun almost immediately, it was several years before the lands could be officially designated as national forests. New Hampshire forester Philip Ayres described the federal purchases in the Whites as being carried out with "remarkable skill. The Government employed as purchasing agent, a red-headed man from Kansas [William L. Hall] who came up our way and beat the Yankees out of their boots in the matter of careful buying." What had to happen was for the state government to enact a law permitting the federal government to buy land. Then the government would buy from willing sellers, for the most part, which meant they had to take what was offered and could not always get the choicest land. Those who thought their property still viable as farmland often wouldn't sell; others sold their land, but cut any standing timber first. Others held on to mineral rights when they sold the land itself. Assembling a national forest was hard work.[56]

The first federal purchase in the White Mountains was Crawford Notch in 1911, consisting of about six thousand acres, and the White Mountain National Forest was formally established in 1918. By 1938 almost 13 percent of New Hampshire's land had been purchased as part of the White Mountain National Forest, at a cost of more than six million dollars. Much of this was the same land that had been sold by the state in 1867 for a mere twenty-six thousand dollars.[57]

In 1920, Philip Ayres waxed romantic about the connections between urban and hinterland landscapes embodied in the White Mountain National Forest: "Here the old lumber camps are in decay. The new forest is springing into life wherever fire has not destroyed the soil. A new patriotism fills [the hiker's] heart, a sense of protecting at the fountain head not only the timber that will give to the people future houses, furniture and tools, but also pure drinking water to many cities, steady power at the wheels of hundreds of factories, and a strong, full flow upon which without interruption the shipping from these cities and factories may pass to and from the sea. What myriads of electric lights throughout New England are dependent upon the steady flow of mountain streams!"[58] Drinking water, industry, and even electric lights owed their security to the trees of New Hampshire. The city and the mountains, Ayres understood, were part of a single, interdependent landscape. The state's seemingly pristine environment is a metropolitan nature, the result of new urban and rural interactions.

The coming of the railroads, the transformation of the agricultural econ-

2.11   Steep, rough terrain on Mount Washington in New Hampshire. Note the
hiker taking a break in the lower right-hand corner of the image. Glass stereographs-
Langenheim-P-2006-33-10 [detail]. Courtesy of the Library Company of Philadelphia.

omy, the influence of the textile industry, and the growing importance of the tourist trade created a new context in which farmers, loggers, industrialists, mill workers, summer visitors, and armchair travelers negotiated a new forested landscape in New Hampshire. These negotiations were the result of a momentary confluence of interests among people and groups of people who had often had competing interests in the past and would again in the future. That the protection of forests would seem a practicable and necessary solution to their many problems should remind us that, as we have already seen in Pennsylvania, the reforestation of the Northeast was never a historical inevitability, and in some places would have seemed quite improbable. Nonetheless, at the same time that the unlikely overlap of various selfish and altruistic motives began to bring back New Hampshire trees, similar negotiations were going on across the Connecticut River in Vermont. Differences in landscape, infrastructure, politics, and imagination meant that the return of Vermont forests came in a different way. Vermonters and their visitors shaped a more domesticated landscape as they brought trees back to their farms, hills, and newly public lands.

CHAPTER THREE

Packaging the Forested Farm in Vermont

Where New Hampshire is rugged and refined, Vermont is homey and pure. Along Highway 89 from Concord to Montpelier, the view changes. In New Hampshire, tall evergreens shroud the road, allowing no vista beyond the trees. Across the Connecticut River in Vermont, the highway rounds a curve and the deep woods drop away as cows and woodlots come into view. The landscape is tidy, not wild. Vermont is the country, not wilderness. And Vermonters have been selling this image to city tourists for over a hundred years.[1]

The domesticated farmscapes visible from Highway 89 mirror the politics, publicity campaigns, and popular perceptions of the state. Vermont, according to its politicians, residents, and tourists, is a bucolic country retreat where life is simple and the land is tamed. Yet the landscape is not simply a mirror of politics and popular perceptions; it has been shaped by them as well. It is tempting to attribute the pastoral image of Vermont to soil types, hill slopes, and elevations. The state, according to this argument, is more pastoral because its land was more easily tamed. But the reality is more complicated. Vermont seems more tamed in part because of soils and hill slopes, but also because of transportation networks, regional markets, local agricultural policies, and federal programs that allowed farms to survive. The dairy products and maple sugar that form the core of Vermont's farming business have been barely enough. Tourism and trees help farmers make ends meet.

Tourism in New Hampshire was about escaping the city for unspoiled nature—to lakes, mountains, and woods—but that is not the image Vermonters have chosen to project. Tourism in Vermont is about escaping the city to experience the farm as retreat. Trees—forests, woodlots, and tree-lined paths—are deliberate components of Vermont as consciously shaped, beautiful farm country that offers respite to harried city dwellers in search of an imagined simpler life.

New Hampshire's program for marketing abandoned farms to tourists was blunt: *Abandoned Farms for Summer Homes* was a beautiful annual publication, and no one expected the rich city people who bought houses in the lake country to take up a hoe or rebuild a barn. The campaign in Vermont was quite different. A 1907 Vermont Board of Agriculture publicity booklet, for example, was titled *Beautiful Vermont: Unsurpassed as a Residence or Playground, For the Summer Resident, The Summer Visitor, The Tourist, The Capitalist and The Workingman*, clearly signaling that Vermont lands remained productive. The booklet's text states firmly: "There are no 'abandoned farms' in Vermont, indeed 70 percent of Vermont farm property is occupied by its owners. There is, however, considerable desirable property for sale at a reasonable price." Some land might appear abandoned, the board insisted, but "the lands are still used for agriculture, however, and the taxes are paid by the owners; in no sense are the farms 'deserted.' To those who are tired of the worry and waste of the town, they still offer a good living under comfortable conditions."[2]

Victor Spear, statistical secretary for the Board of Agriculture, encouraged farmers to jump wholeheartedly into the cultivation of "new crops" at the turn of the century: maple sugar, milk, and tourists.[3] In 1911 the legislature acknowledged the development of the tourist industry as a crucial endeavor for the Vermont economy, and legislators created the Bureau of Publicity instead of relying on the Board of Agriculture to market the state. The first publication of the new bureau was titled *Vermont, Designed by the Creator for the Playground of the Continent*.[4]

3.1 From New Hampshire, looking into Vermont, 1905. "Connecticut River and Brattleboro, Vt., from the east." Library of Congress, Prints & Photographs Division, Detroit Publishing Company Collection, LC-D4-10860.

3.2   Cows among the Vermont trees in Jamaica, Vermont, ca. 1910. From a postcard, photograph most likely taken by H. L. Chapman of Windham, Vermont. Courtesy of Vermont Historical Society.

In addition to encouraging farmers to take in summer boarders, and summer people to buy vacation property in the state, the Vermont Bureau of Publicity, like the Department of Agriculture before it, emphasized the productivity of Vermont farmland. In a 1916 publication, the bureau related the stories of many Vermonters who had taken seemingly unproductive farmland and turned a good profit. Luke Fisher of Cabot, for example, used modern drainage techniques to make his family farm more productive than it had ever been under his father's ownership. C. J. Barbour of Bridport, who had been a mailman, bought five hundred acres and developed a business raising cattle for sale. W. B. Wheelock of Colchester, who had been a laborer in a creamery, bought a small farm, read up on modern farming practices, and made the endeavor a success.⁵ The publicity bureau was not simply marketing inexpensive land, but marketing productive land. Tidy, successful farms were important to a tourist industry that was selling a country experience.

Images in tourist pamphlets, railroad brochures, and travelogues carried a remarkably consistent message. A 1908 advertising booklet for the Echo Lake Hotel in Tyson, for example, drew on what were already common tropes in Vermont vacation literature. Alongside promises of "good beds, cool rooms, no mosquitoes, and a table simple but with food well cooked and served," a photograph captures the carefully crafted image of pastoral Vermont: a wooded path, hardwoods all around, and a cow in a small and pleasant clearing. The caption reads "Description Unnecessary." Who could need a description? The countryside spoke for itself.⁶

The idea of Vermont as a pastoral retreat had already begun to take hold in the late nineteenth century. New Yorker Bertha Oppenheim was one of the early urbanites to fall under its spell. Around 1900, at a dinner party in what was then considered Harlem, she fell in love with the image of Vermont. In her memoir *Winged Seeds*, she reminisces about her first glimpse of the pastoral landscape: her host's vacation photographs, which were passed around the table after dessert. She and her husband Nathan decided on that March evening in their friends' 104th Street studio that Vermont would become their summer home.⁷

She described the images that enthralled her: "There were prints of old

Vergennes on the Otter, with its picturesque falls, its stately elms and maples. There were views of Sleepy Otter Creek and Fort Cassin; views of tree-hung coves, and great, ancient rocks; views of rugged shore lines and still pools; pictures of wind-tossed trees on strange-shaped islands. Always there was the wondrous background of a great lake, of misty hills, and green valleys." When she and her husband finally saw Vermont for themselves that August, they were not disappointed: "New York with its grind, its clamor, its deadly heat seemed like a bad dream. That March night, in Walter's studio was the bridge over which we had passed into another life." When they first stepped off the Lake Champlain steamer ferry onto the Vermont shore, they were greeted by pastoral perfection: "a golden, glowing sunset, with no sound by the water, the wind in the pines, and cowbells far away." The Oppenheims spent their first season in Vermont sleeping in a canvas tent on a dairy farm. Before the summer's end, they had purchased a piece of property and were arranging to raise dairy cows and chickens on their own. "Saints in Heaven!" Bertha wrote. "Was there ever anything so absolutely beautiful! Old oaks and maples, pines, hemlocks, white birches, gray poplars, shagbarks, and cedars, hundreds and hundreds of them; great mossy rocks, a sandy beach sheltered from the north—all this had a view to the west and ranges and ranges of Adirondack hills. Back of the woods, toward the south, was a partially cleared meadow. 'For a garden,' sang my heart. And beyond lay the peaceful, fertile Green Mountain Valley."[8]

Nathan continued his New York City medical practice until about 1910, but he and Bertha spent more and more time in Vermont. They learned about farming, they got to know their neighbors, and they began to feel as though Vermont was their "true" and "spiritual" home. But there was one small "fly that marred the beauty of the amber." Cottages full of city people kept springing up nearby. "Mostly there were people from New York, Brooklyn, and still more distant cities. Rights of way seemed to be everywhere, particularly through our garden and past our porch. Our wonderful peace and solitude was broken in upon." The prevalence of city people brought another annoyance: "The natives were growing sophisticated as to their charges, despite our friendly intercourse. They evidently believed that business and friendship had nothing in common. They cheerfully charged city prices for their produce. To-day, knowing the farmers' problems at first hand, I believe they were absolutely justified in so doing." For Bertha and Nathan, as for many early twentieth-century New Yorkers, Vermont was a world apart. It seemed to be everything the city was not: quiet, beautiful, well-ordered, and full of pleasing scents and picturesque farms. There were three central components to her pastoral ideal: trees, farms, and isolation from the city. "Oaks and maples, pines [and] hemlocks" were as central to Bertha Oppenheim's vision of Vermont as were "cowbells" and the "fertile Green Mountain Valley."[9] The contrast with the city was very much the point.

In Vermont as elsewhere, trees, farms, and cities—though seemingly at odds—were all a part of the same historical processes. By the 1920s Vermont residents and visitors understood that the state's trees and farms were vital components of a unique landscape, an antidote and alternative to all things urban. But as the stories of Pennsylvania and New Hampshire might now lead us to expect, the very same countryside that urbanites sought out in order to leave their chaotic world was in fact only possible because of rural interactions with the city.

Forests had declined in favor of other uses in nineteenth-century Vermont, as they had throughout the Northeast. The peak of land clearing in Vermont came in 1880, when less than a third of the state was in forest.[10] That year, 83 percent of Vermont was in farms, though only 56 percent of the state was classified as "improved" farmland. The rest of the farmland was in woodlots or "other unimproved land," defined by the census as "brush land, rough or stony land, swamp land, and any other land which is not improved or in forest."[11] By 1920, improved farmland had declined to 29 percent. Almost as much, 24 percent of the state's land, was in farm woodlands. By 1990, 75 percent of the state was covered in forests, much of it on farmland.[12]

These new forested landscapes were created in part by Vermont farmers' connections with cities, the character of which changed dramatically in the mid-nineteenth century. Vermont had long been at a disadvantage among the New England states in industrial development, because only Vermont lacked direct access to the sea. In order to get products to or from Vermont

3.3 Important locations in Vermont. Map by Rachel Hope Allison.

farms and mills to the region's busy ports, Vermonters had to depend on long journeys on inland waters. Lake Champlain, on Vermont's western border, offered access to the St. Lawrence River in the north, with its importance to Canadian trade and its access to the ocean. The lake also leads to the Hudson River in the south, with access to Albany and Troy, New York, and on Vermont's eastern border is the Connecticut River, offering access to western Massachusetts.[13] In winter, when the rivers were frozen, access was particularly difficult, and Vermont remained relatively isolated until the coming of the railroads in the 1850s.[14]

Despite this initial isolation, when the railroads arrived, Vermont became a pivotal transportation nexus. It lay in the path of New York and Boston merchants who were seeking Canadian markets and a northern route to the

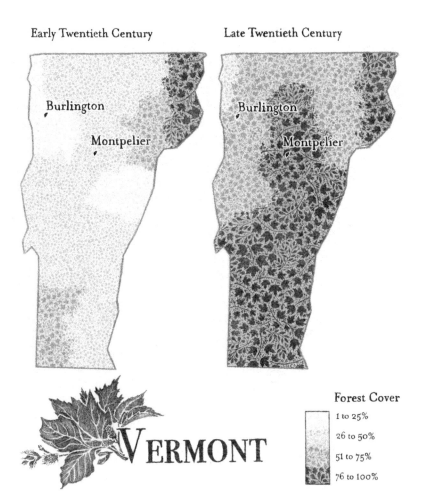

Early Twentieth Century   Late Twentieth Century

Burlington   Burlington

Montpelier   Montpelier

VERMONT

Forest Cover

1 to 25%

26 to 50%

51 to 75%

76 to 100%

3.4   The increase in forest cover in Vermont during the twentieth century.
Map by Rachel Hope Allison.

West. When the Canadian Pacific Railway reached the Pacific in 1885, the New England states had a new route west, through Vermont. In 1923 the Grand Trunk and Canadian Northern Railway systems, brought together in the Canadian National Railways, offered a second Canadian route west. The competition from the new routes served as a check on the rates charged by the New York Central, Pennsylvania, Erie, and Baltimore and Ohio railroads. "Vermont is thus viewed to be a key-stone," wrote railroad historian William J. Wilgus, "a pivotal point—in the northern arch of transportation connecting the continent's interior with New England and incidentally with the port of New York, as a governing influence in the weaving of the two countries' freight rate traffic."[15]

Vermont's first few miles of railroad track were laid in 1848, and a rail-and-steamboat through route was established from New York City to Montreal a year later. Passengers were for the first time able to purchase tickets in either city for any point along the route, which included Vermont. In 1851, when the train route between Boston and the St. Lawrence River was completed, Vermont connected the United States to Canada by rail. By 1900 there were over a thousand miles of railroad tracks in Vermont, connecting Montpelier, Burlington, Bennington, and Brattleboro with Portland, Boston, Albany, and New York City. The competition between rival companies to reach Canada and the West through Vermont led to a plethora of rail routes through the state, with comparatively low freight rates.[16]

Once trains made significant inroads into New England, farmers throughout the region who had been growing market crops that stored well, such as wheat and corn, ran into stiff competition from western farmers. Yet the trains also brought these farmers into closer contact with the region's urban markets, making perishable crops like fruits, vegetables, poultry, and dairy products viable alternatives for keeping a farm profitable. Vermont farmers were uniquely situated to provide the Northeast with milk.

Milk is highly perishable and must be consumed close to the place it is produced. The region that is able to supply fresh milk to a city is referred to as a milkshed, and since milksheds are measured in time, not space, changes in transportation technology affect their size. Limitations on the speed of transportation from farm to market meant that until the mid-nineteenth century, milksheds were very small. Indeed, as late as 1825, many New York City families kept their own dairy cows.[17] Upstate milk was first shipped for sale in New York City in 1836, but it took a while for the distant suppliers to take over the market.[18] In the 1850s there were still twice as many dealers selling milk from urban dairy herds as from upstate farms. The combination of rising urban land values and improvements in transportation and refrigeration eventually led to the disappearance of urban herds in New York City by 1904.[19]

By 1930 Vermont was the major milk supplier in the Northeast. The average northeastern state had 88 milk cows per thousand people; New Hampshire had 166, Maine had 172, and Vermont had 742, almost as many milk cows as people.[20] The Northeast as a whole was relatively self-sufficient in terms of milk and cream, importing only 3 percent of its cream (and no milk) from western farms. In 1934, northeasterners consumed nearly eighteen billion pounds of milk and cream; nearly 95 percent of it was produced on the farms in the area, with about 2 percent coming from cows kept in cities and towns. Still, there was significant movement of milk around the region. The farms of neither New York nor Massachusetts, for example, produced enough milk to support their cities; Vermont, with three cows to every four people, exported three-fourths of its milk to other states.[21]

In 1900, Boston received about a quarter of its milk by wagon from farms within twenty miles of the city; the rest came in by rail. At the time, 140 miles was the farthest shipping point from the city, and Bellows Falls was the only town in Vermont serving the Boston market. By 1915, farms throughout the state were shipping milk to Boston on the Central Vermont Railroad.[22]

Because entrepreneurs in New York and Massachusetts had been eager to build rail lines through Vermont to reach the Canadian lines west, Vermont farmers in the late nineteenth and early twentieth century had unique direct rail access to both New York City and Boston. The dairy farmers of Maine were too far from New York to be able to serve that market with fluid milk, and the rail lines from New Hampshire were too circuitous. Both Maine and New Hampshire served Boston, but only Vermont had the benefit of easy access to the New York City market, too.[23]

By the early twentieth century Vermont farmers, unlike farmers in much of the rest of the Northeast, had carved out a lasting niche for themselves. The same railroads that provided access to urban markets also brought tourists to the state and campaigned to develop Vermont's tourist industry in order to increase ridership. The twenty-first-century Vermont landscape remains a rural landscape—a carefully cultivated rural setting among acres of new trees, offering both agricultural commodities and a countrified fantasy for visitors from the city. Tourism, like milk production, became a crucial element in both the shaping of the landscape and the survival of forested Vermont farms.[24]

Throughout the twentieth century, Vermont enjoyed fewer tourists than other New England states. Even as late as 1950, Vermont brought in less income from seasonal dwellings than any other state in the region.[25] Tourism was nevertheless a significant—and growing—component of the Vermont economy. When the railroads and the Board of Agriculture campaigned to get more tourists to visit the state, they took two tacks: enticing out-of-staters to visit and encouraging Vermont residents to make those visits possible and enjoyable.[26]

Bertha Oppenheim's experience was the kind that the railroads and the agricultural board wanted to promote. When she and her husband arrived in Vermont, they spent their first night in Jim Winans's farmhouse and thereafter camped on his land. Winans was a dairy farmer, and he and his wife supplemented their income by taking in city guests. The Oppenheims were immediately enamored of the Winanses and the farm landscape, though the reality of farm life was not precisely the stuff of dreams. Bertha wrote of their first morning in Vermont: "I think I was dreaming of owning a cow and a horse and chickens and all sorts of delightful things when [Nathan] awakened me for our swim, with which we began our day. The day was young as were we. . . . We found Jim Winans in the barn, milking his cows. They were grades, part Guernsey, part Ayrshire. But we did not know it then—they were just plain cows to us both. The barn was rather smelly, and, I fear, very messy. This was before the time of big, co-operative milk plants, Cooperative Agricultural Agents, and scientific supervision of farms."[27] Bertha had enjoyed the picturesque farm; the working farm was a bit more problematic.

The Oppenheims may have found the Winans farm through railroad advertising literature. As early as 1891, the railroads in Vermont were hard at work wooing both city tourists and Vermont farmers to be their hosts. The Central Vermont Railroad, for example, solicited listings from farmers who were willing to take in boarders, and that year published the names and addresses of people who were willing to do so in a richly illustrated booklet called *Summer Homes Among the Green Hills of Vermont and Along the Shores of Lake Champlain*, which was distributed in cities throughout the Northeast.[28] The booklet was updated numerous times over the next couple of decades.

The railroad took great care to emphasize that the farmers listed in the booklet, while true farmers, were also cultivated people who could provide a charming retreat: "The homes of these Vermont people are the homes of a forceful, wide-awake and educated population that read the daily New York and Boston papers, take the magazines and buy the best books of the day." Nevertheless, "all of the places advertised have plenty of milk, cream, butter and eggs. The country is richly productive and the summer fare of fruit, vegetable, eggs and poultry is perfect."[29] The railroad brochure strove to erase all evidence of work—the pastoral landscape was not a landscape of labor, but of cultivated leisure. The farmers who welcomed boarders were "all well-to-do people, own their own farms and take city boarders more for the enjoyment of it than for the revenue they receive out of it."[30]

Many Vermont farmers, like the Winanses, enthusiastically embraced the strategy, actively participating in the creation of a country experience for city guests. The Dole family in Danville, Vermont, for example, included marketing to tourists in its strategy for maintaining the farm. When William Dole inherited the farm from his parents in the late nineteenth century, his primary income was from his large herd of dairy cows and his grove of maple trees. When his son George inherited the farm in the first part of the twentieth century, he continued to produce milk for the Boston market until the 1950s. By that time, however, the country experience had become the farm's primary product. George and Ethel Dole made their income by taking guests

3.5 "Fairmount," a farmhouse taking in boarders in South Londonderry, Vermont, in the early twentieth century. Later photographic postcards of the same house suggest that the owners continued to take in boarders at least through the summer of 1920. Note the stone wall in the foreground, suggesting rocky fields previously cleared for agriculture. Such walls have since become a common sight throughout northeastern woods, visible evidence of the land's former agricultural use. Courtesy of the Vermont Historical Society.

into their home, serving home-cooked lunches in their dining room, and selling maple-nut fudge at a roadside stand.[31]

By 1922 the image of Vermont as a bucolic retreat was set. Photographer and travel writer Wallace Nutting documented the pastoral vision of Vermont in *Vermont Beautiful*, the first in his series of travel and photography books. "Some years ago," Nutting wrote, "the author traveled two hundred miles through a fine agricultural country without seeing anything sufficiently picturesque to call for a pause. But this cannot be done in Vermont. Here is the state of the ideal farm." Vermont farms, he continued, can answer "the dreams of those millions who have, or intend sometime to have, a place to feed their souls as well as their bodies."[32]

Nutting, as a photographer, knew very well the importance of image. He encouraged Vermonters to go further in their packaging of the landscape: "These farms can be named. What city man would not pay almost double for a place well named?" City people, he advised, should spend as much time in the restorative country as possible: "The reader should not infer, however, that the author imagines no good can come out of the city. The city is a necessary evil, and the master mind in banking, trade, and government is compelled to work from the city as a center. But more and more that master mind requires the tonic of country air, and the rugged independence fostered by country life."[33]

Vermont farmers, too, benefited from city people purchasing country places, Nutting explained: "One can tell at a glance whether a farm is real, in the sense of being a self-sustaining enterprise, or whether it is owned by a summer resident. Increasingly our Eastern farms are going into the hands of those who play with them rather than live by them. This is well for the neighboring farmer in that it furnishes him with lucrative odd jobs, for we admit that the city buyer does not stint funds in the development of his farming hobby, so that it has been wittily said that the difference between the agriculturist and a farmer is, that the one puts his money into the land while the other takes his money out."[34]

This persistent farming economy, intertwined as it was with urban markets and dependent as it was on urban tourists, provided the context in which

Vermont's forests returned. As we have already seen elsewhere in the Northeast, the new forested landscape of twentieth-century Vermont was not accidental, but the result of new and overlapping needs in the city and country that made standing forests valuable again. By the 1880s, after over a hundred years of intensive farming on cleared land coupled with aggressive clearing of pine for lumber, much of the Vermont forest was gone. Some estimates put the late-nineteenth-century percentage of forest cover in Vermont as low as 25 percent; others as high as 38 percent. Whatever the percentage, a majority of what remained was hardwood.

Vermont, with its lower elevations and richer soils, had always been more hospitable to hardwoods than New Hampshire or Maine. Nevertheless, pine forests had originally lined the Connecticut River and the banks of Lake Champlain, and the Green Mountains had been largely covered by spruce. By 1880, most of the pine had been cut for Burlington's lumber market—the nation's third largest, behind Albany and Chicago. The majority of the lumber sold in Burlington was not harvested in Vermont; it came from Maine, Michigan, and Canada on rivers and lakes as logs, which were then milled into boards and sent to eastern markets by train. Even after the virtual exhaustion of Vermont's pine, the state had a peak harvest of 384 million board feet in 1890, about three-quarters in spruce. Thereafter, with the spruce supplies sharply down as well, the local timber industry turned its attention to hardwoods—mostly maple and birch, and some oak, ash, and chestnut—used primarily for boxes, furniture, veneers, cooperage stock, and other manufactured items. Second-growth spruce was in demand for both lumber and paper pulp.[35]

In 1882, in response to fears of deforestation, the legislature appointed a committee to study the state's forests and, in 1892, established the Vermont Forestry Commission. Before the end of the next decade, Vermont had both a fledgling state forest system and a state nursery, and when the forest commission hired its first professional forester in 1909 they turned to Austin Hawes, an expert in nursery plantings who had previously been the state forester of Connecticut.[36]

Hawes described his chosen field of forestry as "a new branch of agriculture

3.6 Mid-twentieth-century forests of Vermont. Aerial view across the Somerset Watershed. United States Forest Service Region 9, photograph R9_501463. Courtesy of the Forest History Society.

in this country that is as yet but little understood."[37] Like Pennsylvania's Mira Dock, he believed his primary duty as state forester was to teach the people of Vermont that forestry was agriculture. He wanted Vermonters to "consider the forest as an agricultural crop to be harvested, reseeded, improved, and reaped again; instead of a mine to be exploited and abandoned." Watershed protection and timber resource development were the primary uses of the timber crop, he wrote, but the "value in preserving the beauty of the State's scenery is not to be overlooked, and this will undoubtedly be more of a commercial asset of the State in the future than it has been in the past."[38]

New property tax laws in Vermont specifically encouraged tree planting,

3.7 "The Passing Shower, Green Mountains [between 1900 and 1906]." Fields, woodlots, and forested vistas were all part of the picturesque landscapes drawing tourists to Vermont. State Forester Austin Hawes described the state's scenery as a valuable "commercial asset." Library of Congress, Prints & Photographs Division, Detroit Publishing Company Collection, LC-D4-16032.

especially by farmers. In 1912, the legislature passed several laws exempting standing timber from personal property taxes and ensuring low real property tax assessments on land that had been planted in trees. The seedlings couldn't be just any trees; they had to be of species approved by the state forester and planted according to his recommendations. In those early years, the state of Vermont was distributing both seedlings and planting advice for free.[39]

After removal of spruce and pine from Vermont farmers' woodlots, light-tolerant hardwoods were the first to move in; the commercially lucrative soft-woods required planting. Vermont's forestry commission was the fourth (after New York, Pennsylvania, and Connecticut) to engage in an aggressive tree nursery program and tree planting campaign. When the state nursery opened in Burlington in 1908, it brought in 130 pounds of white pine seed from New York, in addition to importing thousands of white pine seedlings from Germany. In 1909 and 1910, the state nursery sold over a half million seedlings to landowners throughout the state and planted many acres of state-owned land. Most of what was planted in those years was European white pine, grown from seedlings. The rest was Norway spruce, imported from Europe, with a scattering of Scotch pine, red pine, and locust seedlings.[40]

After blister rust was discovered on the white pine seedlings from Germany, no more European trees were used, and the nursery turned from white pine to Scotch pine. By 1918 the nursery was growing no more white pine. Scotch pine was widely distributed until 1930, when it became apparent that most of the trees were growing so crooked as to be of little use for lumber, and the nursery turned to red pine instead. The Scotch and red pine found in Vermont today are a direct result of regional and international migrations of both trees and tree disease.[41]

In the state agricultural report for 1920 through 1922, Vermont's chief forester W. G. Hastings and his colleague E. S. Brigham reported that since the state forestry department had been created in 1909, Vermont had acquired almost thirty thousand acres of state forests and had overseen the planting of about eight million trees.[42] That means that in 1922, in a state of almost six million acres—one of the smallest states in the union—only about 0.5 percent of the land was in public woods. While eight million trees may sound like a lot—the state's forest nurseries had given away six hundred thousand seedlings or more each year to help landowners reforest woodlots and roadsides—it was not very much. At a thousand trees per acre (a reasonable density for replanting a former pasture in pine, for example), eight million trees could have stocked only about 12.5 square miles—this in a tiny state in which there were nevertheless more than 1,500 square miles of denuded or poorly forested land that needed the little plants. "It will take at least one thousand million trees to plant such an area," reported Hastings. It would mean planting forty million trees a year for twenty-five years to get the job done, and in no year had more than one million seedlings been sent out.[43]

While Vermont was behind other states in replanting efforts and forestry expenditures—New York led the region, and Connecticut and New Hampshire both distributed far more trees as well—the challenge was the same throughout the Northeast. Most states promised free or at-cost seedlings to all those who wanted them, and state nurseries could not keep up with demand. Educational efforts outstripped supply. And with private landowners scrambling to follow the dictates of modern forestry, there simply weren't enough young trees to be had to properly plant all the scraggly, underused acres in tidy rows of spruce and pine. Even though demand for seedlings regularly outstripped supply throughout the Northeast and little land, in any absolute sense, was actively replanted with state nursery stock, the free

3.8 This meadow, on the grounds of the Marsh-Billings-Rockefeller National Historical Park, is "flanked by a historic plantation of Norway spruce (*Picea abies*), dated 1887, at right; and a plantation of European larch (*Larix decidua*), also dated 1887, at left." Library of Congress, Prints & Photographs Division, Historic American Buildings Survey/Historic American Engineering Record, Marsh-Billings-Rockefeller National Historical Park Collection, HALS VT-1-31.

3.9   An 1876 woodshed being taken over by late twentieth-century trees and scrub near the Mount Tom Forest in Vermont. The Historic American Buildings Survey text associated with this photograph explains that "the view includes the open woodcutting yard (now a meadow), and the woodshed (surviving); the saw shed on the meadow was long ago demolished." Library of Congress, Prints & Photographs Division, Historic American Buildings Survey/Historic American Engineering Record, Marsh-Billings-Rockefeller National Historical Park Collection, HALS VT-1-19.

tree programs were an important and influential part of the early twentieth-century forestry campaigns. People were hungry for the trees, worked to protect them, and wanted to improve on nature's gifts.

For all that, much of the colorful foliage that tourists have long associated with Vermont comes not from farm woodlots of pine or spruce or from state forests restocked with evergreens, but from a tree crop carefully cultivated by farmers, with help from natural succession, to serve both tourists and urban food markets: groves of sugar maples. Timber cultivation could offer farmers both scenery for tourists and an extra source of income when it was time to harvest, but the understory of sugar maples left behind after the lucrative pine and spruce had been cut away offered an annual, tangible contribution to farm income: sap.

Maple syrup is condensed sap, and maple sugar is made by continuing to cook the sap until it condenses into solid form. Early settlers in Vermont learned sugaring techniques from Native Americans, and the settlers depended on maple sugar and syrup for their sugar supply in the seventeenth and eighteenth centuries. By the late nineteenth century, though, with cane sugar more commonly and cheaply available, maple syrup and maple sugar had become luxury items.[44] In the early twentieth century, modern collection and processing technologies and distribution networks made the industry more profitable.

The sugar maple tree, sometimes called the hard or rock maple, has a very specific range: it grows almost exclusively in the eastern United States and Canada. The tree is prevalent as far west as the edge of the Plains, but the foothills of Vermont's Green Mountains, with their moderate elevations, cold spring nights, and warm days, are among the few places in the United States where maple syrup of high quality can be produced consistently.[45] Though maple trees were tapped throughout the state, the northern counties of Orleans, Franklin, and Caledonia were the top maple sugar and syrup producing counties in the early twentieth century.[46]

The process of making maple syrup and sugar is tricky. The season is short, generally lasting from two to eight weeks, and the amount of syrup made from a single grove of trees is quite small.[47] According to a Vermont

3.10 "Gathering Sap at a Maple Sugar Camp" in Vermont, between 1900 and 1906. Library of Congress, Prints & Photographs Division, Detroit Publishing Company Collection, LC-D4-19210.

Agricultural Experiment Station publication from 1928, "Although it is an important crop in some localities and its total value impressive, it is a side line rather than a staple crop even within the producing territory."[48] The sap of the sugar maple can only be collected during the short period in the spring when the nights are below freezing and the days are warm. The perfect weather for sugaring has an overnight temperature of 25 degrees Fahrenheit and a daytime temperature of 55 degrees, with damp northerly winds.[49] A cold day or a warm night stops the flow until the proper conditions return.[50] Because of the short, intense season, most maple groves were small in scale and run by farmers who also produced other commodities for market.[51] In 1912, the Vermont Maple Sugar Makers' Association explained that vulnerability to weather was offset by farm diversity and the strength of urban demand for the products: "A shift of the wind; a change in temperature or humidity and especially a change of barometer pressure, which is the actual force behind a rapid flow of sap, may turn a big sap day into a complete fiasco . . . but [the farmer] may charge all this up in his profit and loss account along with his products of milk and cream for the city contractor. . . . It should be borne in mind by the town consumer that the farm price demanded has never been exorbitant for any product."[52] Maple groves and dairy farming went hand in hand.

In 1860, New York was the leading state in maple product production, though lumbering had taken a toll on the industry there by 1900, as maple groves were cut down for making shoe lasts. Nineteenth-century lumbering for hardwood floors, toothpicks, ship keels, and furniture placed demands on the sugar bushes in Illinois, Indiana, and Michigan as well.[53] Once again, Vermont's relative isolation shaped its landscape: Vermont maple groves were not close enough to industry centers to be threatened until much later, at which point maple products had become a more lucrative specialty product. A pamphlet published by the Vermont Maple Sugar Makers' Association that year explained that maple sugar "has already passed the point of being considered a necessity and its use is now limited to those who can afford it as a luxury; even the poorest quality the price per pound will purchase several pounds of cane sugar for home use. Thus the poor farmer cannot use it except as a delicacy."[54]

3.11 "At Work in a Maple Sugar Camp" in Vermont, 1906. Library of Congress, Prints & Photographs Division, Detroit Publishing Company Collection, LC-D4-19212.

In the early twentieth century, most farmers sold their maple products directly to consumers. Those who wanted a wholesale market for their sugar and syrup could turn to George Cary in St. Johnsbury, in northern Vermont. Cary dealt mostly with Vermont farmers, and outside of his business, wholesale distribution of maple sugar was quite small.[55] According to the lore of the maple sugar industry, Cary single-handedly created the wholesale market for maple sugar through folly and accident. Since maple sugar keeps longer than maple syrup, farmers in the late nineteenth century boiled down what syrup couldn't be sold quickly into sugar for later sale.[56] It was used as a table sweetener and to flavor other syrups, but there was more sugar than demand. Apparently, in the 1890s, Cary, a wholesale grocery salesman from Maine, accepted fifteen hundred pounds of maple sugar in exchange for a grocery order.[57] There was no market for the sugar, and Cary's boss was livid. Desperately searching for a buyer, Cary talked a tobacco manufacturer into using maple sugar instead of cane sugar as a sweetener and preservative. He sold the maple sugar for half a penny less a pound than the cane sugar cost, but even then he had to bargain hard. Years later, Cary remembered: "Finally, I told him that if he would buy my fifteen hundred pounds I would agree to sell one hundred boxes of his plug tobacco on my next Vermont trip; but he was a cautious soul and would take only two hundred pounds of my sugar." The small amount worked out well, Cary reported, and soon the tobacco manufacturer came back for the rest. Over the next several years, demand from the tobacco industry grew such that Cary moved from Maine to Vermont, and in 1904 he founded the Cary Maple Sugar Company, a wholesale maple sugar distributorship.[58]

Until World War II, when cane sugar rationing sent prices for maple sugar skyrocketing, the tobacco industry purchased most of Cary's supply. But by the time cigarette manufacturers stopped sweetening their product with maple, Cary was well-placed to move into the luxury sugar market. Over the course of the latter half of the twentieth century, the business Cary founded in St. Johnsbury expanded to include not just a large distributorship, but a museum, a gift shop, and living history programs, along with a thriving mail order business.[59] H. H. Chadwick, in his 1944 study of the Vermont tourist business, explained what Cary and his successors had learned: "As cars were improved and prices lowered, the masses began to move along the highways. Vacation trips gradually came to be the custom and railroad patronage suffered. Notably, after the World War, after 1918, there was a rapid rise in touring and vacation business boomed. Tourist home signs multiplied and there was rapid growth in the number of overnight cabins, rural tea rooms, roadside filling stations and offerings of vegetables, maple products, apples, honey, and other wares."[60] Maple products, farm stands, and rural tea rooms were all part of a carefully cultivated landscape that Vermont farmers were marketing to travelers, no longer the urban elites who escaped the city by train but a newly mobile class of tourists who owned cars.[61]

Those tourists have been seeing an ever-increasing number of colorful maple leaves as they traverse the state's roads. Estimates from early land surveys suggest that sugar maples made up about 15 percent of Vermont's northern forests three centuries ago; twentieth-century estimates place the number at closer to a quarter of the trees. But their greater abundance—both relative and absolute—is not because farmers have planted maple trees. Sugar maples are present in such numbers for two reasons. First, their value to farmers and tourists as standing trees, and their relative lack of appeal to loggers in search of pine and spruce, meant they managed to escape the timber harvests that claimed so many other trees. Second, as a species they do very well in conditions that are challenging to other trees. Because sugar maples can resprout when cut, produce many seeds, and grow both in shade and in open spaces, they have been able to thrive where many other trees have struggled. Hemlock, for example, needs shade to grow well and has had a much harder time reestablishing itself on cleared Vermont land.[62]

Nevertheless, in most of Vermont, farm woodlots and maple groves have brought forests back to the state. In the steepest and rockiest regions, however, even the combination of dairying, maple sugar, and tourism was not enough for farmers to get by. And so it was a different kind of labor that brought trees back to the Green Mountains and secured their future there. Recreation and flood control were the driving forces behind the creation of the White Mountain National Forest in New Hampshire in the 1920s.

Vermont's national forest owes its origins to a Depression Era need for work. The Green Mountain National Forest was purchased, planted, and groomed in the 1930s, offering jobs and financial relief when little else could.

In Vermont and New Hampshire, the federal government purchased future national forest from local landowners, purchases made possible by the Weeks Act to protect navigable waterways. By the time Vermonters turned to the federal government for reforestation help, protecting navigable waterways was not the only route forward. The 1924 Clarke-McNary Act had expanded the allowable reasons for federal land purchases in the East, permitting timber resource protection and development to be taken into account, since they were arguably as crucial to interstate commerce as the rivers and certainly made more land eligible for federal control.[63]

In 1925, the Vermont legislature passed an act authorizing the U.S. Forest Service to purchase land anywhere in Vermont for national forest. The first purchases were not made until 1931, when the National Forest Reservation Commission authorized the purchase of 31,228 acres in southern Vermont.[64] President Herbert Hoover officially set aside the land as a national forest in 1932.[65] By July 1939, 160,000 acres had been purchased, and plans were in the works to purchase an additional 340,000 acres. Otto Koenig, the national forest supervisor for Vermont, explained that "arbitrary condemnation is not used, land is acquired only from owners who wish to sell."[66] He explained the rationale for the forest: "There is hardly a town or community in Vermont which does not have one or more wood-using industries dependent upon a plentiful supply of high quality timber for raw material. The maintenance of these industries is the principal objective of timber management work in the Green Mountain National Forest. Many thousand acres of second growth have been improved by the thinning, cutting and pruning designed to improve the forest. Trees which are misshapen or in poor health are removed, leaving healthy, rapidly growing stands of timber. Some 800 acres of old abandoned fields have been planted with young nursery grown trees."[67]

In 1933, the *Vermonter* magazine reported thirteen forestry camps in the state, "ten on state property and three on national reservations, for unemployed young men, mostly from the cities."[68] The landscape itself was being

3.12   This view of a Vermont town from a forested hillside is of Woodstock Village, Vermont, from Billings Park, a town park adjacent to the Marsh-Billings-Rockefeller National Historical Park. Library of Congress, Prints & Photographs Division, Historic American Buildings Survey/ Historic American Engineering Record, Marsh-Billings-Rockefeller National Historical Park Collection, HALS VT-1-32.

shaped by and for city labor. And when nature enthusiasts enjoyed the trails built by the urban laborers, they did not need to fear being too far from civilization. As Koenig explained, "The delights of forest and trail are all yours in the Vermont National Forest continually traversed by helpful forest rangers."[69]

Vermont residents were initially enthusiastic about the creation of the Green Mountain National Forest, but they soon became concerned that the federal government was going too far, grabbing too much of Vermont's land, taking it out of the tax base and assuming control of too many resources. In addition to establishing a Vermont national forest in the 1930s and pushing to expand it, the federal government and out-of-state activists were pushing for a national park, a parkway, and aggressive flood control programs.[70] Land for all of these projects was to be acquired in part through voluntary sales of farms to the federal government and in part through the newly created Resettlement Administration, through which farmers on poor land would be relocated to better areas.

Although condemnation was not a method approved for land acquisition, eminent domain was often used at the last stage of land acquisitions, since title searches in Vermont were often lengthy and complicated procedures. The use of eminent domain was purely a bureaucratic procedure after farmers and federal agents had already agreed to terms of purchase or relocation, but its use fueled a fear that state legislation authorizing the national forest might allow the federal government to grab control of land indiscriminately. Fears of loss of local control were also fed by the fact that, initially, the Green Mountain National Forest was run administratively from the offices of the White Mountain National Forest in New Hampshire.[71]

Vermonters resisted the expanding federal role in local land management and politics, campaigning both for keeping land ownership within the state and for keeping the wrong kind of tourists out. Opponents of the parkway, in particular, argued that Vermont's success as a tourist idyll depended on peaceful farm and woodland landscapes that too many automobile tourists would destroy. Despite ambitious plans by the Resettlement Administration to relocate people from thousands of acres of submarginal farmland, local opposition meant no Vermont park or parkway land was acquired that way. Ultimately, the plans for the parkway were defeated in the legislature and in local referendums; without the parkway, the federal government abandoned plans for a park. The federal government's land management role in Vermont was instead restricted to the national forest. Vermont would remain a refuge from city life for urban tourists, with no parkway to pollute its carefully safeguarded image as bucolic, remote, and pristine.[72]

By 1940, 240,000 reforested acres of Vermont were in public hands: 160,000 in the Green Mountain National Forest, 70,000 in state forests and parks, and another 10,000 acres owned by municipalities.[73] Since 1940, those public holdings have continued to grow. Throughout the twentieth century, however, the vast majority of Vermont's reforested land was in the form of farm woodlots, apple orchards, and maple groves. As late as 1994, when almost a half million acres of Vermont's forests were in public hands, almost 4 million acres were privately held by over 80,000 individuals, most of whom were farmers or homeowners with fewer than 10 acres of woods.[74] The landscape of twentieth-century Vermont had become a mosaic of forests, woodlots, and farms, all seemingly isolated from the cities of the Northeast and yet intimately connected with urban places far outside the state.

Years after writing *Winged Seeds*, New Yorker Bertha Oppenheim again explained her love of Vermont and again emphasized the interconnectedness of farms and trees: "I think best of all I love trees and woods, silence and sound. I love the peace and the silence of my life on the farm. I love my dogs and my colts and my calves. I love the barns at feeding time. I love the thousand-voiced silence of pine woods at night, the ringing silence of snow-filled woods."[75] The trees and the farm, Bertha's antidotes to urban life, were of one piece with the urban landscape she was escaping. The "thousand-voiced silence of the pine woods" existed, in large part, because she was there to hear it.

3.13 View of a stone wall through the woods of the Marsh-Billings-Rockefeller National Historical Park. Library of Congress, Prints & Photographs Division, Historic American Buildings Survey/Historic American Engineering Record, Marsh-Billings-Rockefeller National Historical Park Collection, HALS VT-1-24.

CHAPTER FOUR

Who Owns Maine's Trees?

I n May 1895, Cornelia "Fly Rod" Crosby sat tying flies in a Maine cabin, admiring the mounted deer and moose heads that adorned the cabin walls and handing out pamphlets to passersby. The cabin was a modest one, a mere ten-by-thirteen-foot structure of peeled logs, but it caught everyone's eye. In the woods of Maine, it would have been no strange sight; in Manhattan's Madison Square Garden, it was decidedly odd.[1]

The cabin and a nearby lean-to, both decorated with antlers, stuffed rabbits, birds, fish, snowshoes, and guns, were part of the Maine exhibit at the first annual New York City Sportsmen's Exhibition. Crosby, an expert hunter and fisher and a tireless promoter of tourism in her home state, was part of the official Maine delegation to the show, and she reveled in showing New Yorkers what life in Maine could be like. For four days, she and her friends Ed Grant and James Mathieson, both Maine hunting guides, handed out leaflets and magazines touting Maine as the "playground of a nation" and demonstrating their backwoods skills. They were a hit and returned to Maine in high spirits with even grander plans for 1896. That next year, they borrowed a specially made railroad car to bring live fish for the display.[2]

In Vermont, forests were entangled with an image of romantic farm retreats; in Maine, they were tied to the romance of the wild. The Maine woods were harsh, as Henry David Thoreau had discovered on his own travels there in 1846: "Nature here was something savage and awful, though beautiful. . . . This was that Earth of which we have heard, made out of Chaos and Old Night."[3] The chaotic harshness had an appeal. When "Fly Rod," Grant, and Mathieson packaged the Maine landscape for New York tourists, they offered a challenge. The Maine woods promised rough living, large game, elusive trout, largemouth bass, and wild excitement. Maine was a place to get lost in the woods, to live off the land, to hone skills with rod and gun and knife.

Or so it seemed. This image of rugged individualism belied a different reality: Crosby was marketing her Manhattan Maine cabin as part of her state's effort to restrict and control the public use of land. The Chamber of Commerce wanted New Yorkers and other urban swells to come to Maine not to set out on their own in the woods but to hire guides who would manage their experiences in hunting camps. They would bring money into the state, but without threatening the valuable forests owned by the giant timber companies.

Fannie Hardy, a naturalist and also an avid hiker and hunter, thought Crosby had it all wrong. More tourists in Maine would mean more rules and more regulations—rules like hunting seasons—that would make it harder for the people of Maine to make use of resources that were rightly theirs. Traditionally, Maine residents had access to timber company land for hiking and hunting; urban tourists who didn't know what they were doing—urban tourists who shot more deer than they could carry, who set fires that burned out of control—they were a problem, not an opportunity.[4]

Olive Cousins couldn't have cared less about tourists. She just wished the state of Maine could manage what little public land it supposedly had under its control. Cousins described herself as a woman with struggles. The state considered her a "pauper," the kind of person that public lands should help support. To her neighbors, Cousins was a "loose woman" and a "nuisance," using land and trees that were more rightfully theirs.[5]

These three women—Cornelia "Fly Rod" Crosby, Fannie Hardy, and Olive Cousins—bring into high relief the ways in which forest property in

4.1   The Maine Exhibit at the New York Sportsman's Show in 1897, the third year "Fly Rod" Crosby set up a log cabin in Madison Square Garden. Although she is not shown in this image, she was at the show and is credited with designing the exhibit. She was working for the Maine Central Railroad at the time. Collections of Phillips Historical Society, courtesy of Maine Historical Society. Maine Memory Network item 17572.

4.2 "Fly Rod" Crosby (*right*), fishing from a canoe with another fisherman on Maine's Moosehead Lake, near Mt. Kineo, ca. 1895. Collections of Maine Historical Society. Maine Memory Network item 15315.

Maine in the early twentieth century was no easy thing to understand, much less manage or control. For Crosby, the Maine woods were an opportunity for statewide economic development; for Hardy, they were a resource for local use; for Cousins, the woods were a lifeline when no other was offered. And the state failed them all.

In Maine, forests were not protectors of urban watersheds: there were no major cities in the state, and the trees were too far upstream from New York, Boston, or Philadelphia to seem important to urban waters at the time. The forest land was not set aside for tourist vistas: most city tourists traveled to the rocky coast, not the vast inland woods, and when they dared venture to the timberlands, the city interlopers with few backwoods skills were seen as a threat, not a boon, for the trees. And the woods were not symbols of a pastoral life: while Maine forests may have been crucial for sustaining country life, the existence they made possible was no pastoral ideal.

Because Maine's north woods were too remote from the shaping influences of the city, and because urban forces were therefore unable to shape the Maine woods as they had elsewhere in the region, forestry was left to the corporations. That means that twenty-first century forests in Maine are under far greater threat. Maine was never deforested to the extent of the rest of the Northeast. Nineteenth- and early twentieth-century Maine continued to see a thriving timber industry, even as the rest of the region feared a timber famine and took steps to stave off a future without trees. In the twenty-first century, when millions of acres of forest land are protected in the hinterland of the northeastern cities, the distant woods of Maine are still being cut. Cities protected forests elsewhere, but couldn't reach far enough into Maine.

The difficulty of managing remote forest land has shaped land ownership patterns in Maine from the state's first years. When Maine separated from Massachusetts in 1820, the older state retained ownership of many unsettled acres in Maine, despite having given up legal jurisdiction. Once the land was settled, or at least arguably so, then Massachusetts's authority over the parcels would finally end. That legal quirk meant that speedy distribution of the public domain seemed to be the simplest way for Maine to clarify its control over all of the lands within its legal boundaries. By 1853, the Commonwealth of Massachusetts no longer owned any land in Maine, and by the 1880s, Maine itself owned only a handful of lots. Some of the public domain had been distributed to farmers, but the vast majority of Maine's acreage had been transferred to a few large landholders with interests in the timber trades.[6]

That meant two things for Maine: First, just as forest conservation was becoming a local and national concern, Maine no longer owned its forests. Second, though the Commonwealth of Massachusetts no longer owned any land in Maine, many Massachusetts (and New York and Connecticut and

MAINE

Baxter State Park

E Plantation

Mount Katahdin

Augusta

White Mountain National Forest

Acadia National Park

Portland

4.3   Important locations in Maine. Map by Rachel Hope Allison.

Pennsylvania) businessmen did. Despite appearances to the contrary, Maine had not rid itself of out-of-state ownership and control.

A century later, the only two significant public landholdings in Maine were the result not of state or national authority being exerted to carve out such spaces, as happened elsewhere in the region. Both Acadia National Park and Baxter State Park were made possible through private gifts. Baxter was a gift to the state from a wealthy former governor; Acadia, located on Mount Desert Island, was created by tourists who were wealthier than those courted by "Fly Rod" Crosby.

Crosby had been marketing Maine to the upper middle class, but Acadia served the very rich. By 1880, Mount Desert Island, which had been popularized by painters Thomas Cole and Frederic Church, had over thirty inns and was a nationally known resort. In the next decades, Rockefellers, Morgans, Fords, Astors, Vanderbilts, Carnegies, and Pulitzers vacationed there.

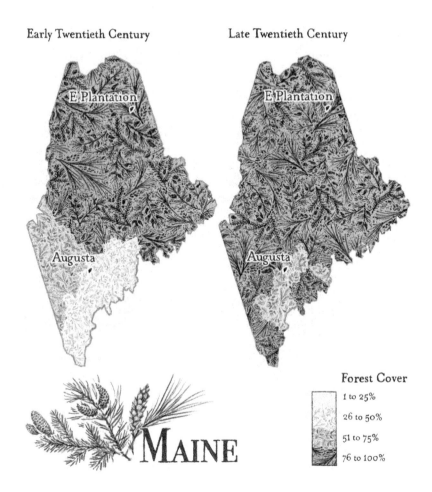

Early Twentieth Century   Late Twentieth Century

E Plantation

Augusta

MAINE

Forest Cover

1 to 25%

26 to 50%

51 to 75%

76 to 100%

4.4 The increase in forest cover in Maine during the twentieth century.
Map by Rachel Hope Allison.

In 1919, this group, led by Harvard president Charles W. Eliot and Boston nature lover and philanthropist Charles B. Dorr, created Acadia National Park, the first national park east of the Mississippi. Wealthy vacation homeowners had created a land trust in 1901 to safeguard against unwanted development in their vacation paradise. By 1916, the trust had six thousand acres and was designated a national monument. In 1919, with fifteen thousand acres, it became a national park, offering permanent federal protection for land that was critically close to the playground of the rich. It was to be a rare reserve of Maine forestland kept from intensive corporate use.[7]

Maine's only other parcel of public land of any significant size—Baxter State Park—was also a gift. While Acadia's first acres were safeguarded from development in order to preserve the views and playgrounds of a group of millionaire vacationers, Baxter State Park was created by a single individual with an affection for the landscape and a passion for wildlife.

Percival P. Baxter, a Maine state representative and state senator in the early years of the twentieth century, was governor of Maine from 1920 to 1925.[8] During and after his tenure, he tried to persuade the legislature to buy the area around Mount Katahdin for a public park. The largest timber companies vehemently opposed the plan, because it would take potentially valuable timberland out of production, and because they thought they could manage the land better than the state. Baxter saw the concentration of timberland ownership in the hands of a small number of corporations as a threat to the landscape, the economy, and the government of Maine. In 1921, he wrote: "These large ownerships create a great monopoly, which controls prices, dictates terms to the owners of small areas, stifles competition, and at times dominates State legislation by means of their arrogant lobbies. The powerful business and political connections of these great corporations, together with their undoubted control of the supply and distribution of news print paper, gives them a position of extraordinary influence over the many activities of the state."[9] He wasn't wrong.

When Baxter couldn't persuade the legislature to make the purchase, he bought the land himself and donated it to the state. He purchased the first 5,960 acres in 1930, including the mountain, and donated the land in 1931.

In 1933, the parcels were officially designated Baxter State Park. Baxter continued to purchase and donate land for the park throughout his life, making his final gift of 7,764 acres in 1962. The park eventually came to encompass 204,733 acres, the largest publicly owned parcel in Maine by far.[10]

By the time Baxter made his first purchase in 1930, 85 percent of the forestland in the state was owned by thirty-two people or firms. Those firms were producing almost a million tons of wood pulp for paper products annually, about 20 percent of the nation's total. In Maine, in contrast to the rest of the Northeast, the twentieth-century forests were corporate forests, and the trees were not scenery, not protectors of watersheds, not symbols of wildness or of country life. They were raw materials for an expanding industry. As urban markets for newsprint, board paper, book paper, and wrapping paper boomed, timber companies consolidated their ownership of the Maine woods, if not their control.[11]

Crosby, Hardy, Cousins, and other Mainers like them maneuvered in the areas where both corporate and government control were always just out of reach. In addition to being so distant from cities and their influence, Maine has a unique history of governance and land management. Alone among the northeastern states, Maine's land office made an early attempt to distinguish between lands that were suitable for agriculture and those suitable only for timber production, and made the lands available on different terms. Since separating from Massachusetts in 1820, Maine has designated some lands as "wildlands," a special category that has had important implications for ownership patterns and management policies in the nineteenth and twentieth centuries. The wildlands were particularly valuable as timberland, and because they were seen as less dependent on state services than agricultural land, they were taxed at a lower rate. In addition, the wildland lots were owned in undivided shares, which meant that while ownership became fragmented through inheritance and sales, the parcels themselves did not. An owner or group of owners with a controlling interest in a wildland parcel could determine what was done with the land.[12] Ultimately, this left Maine officials in the unique position of trying to manage forests by attempting to regulate a small number of large, private corporate owners.[13]

Over the course of the nineteenth century, the Board of Agriculture and the legislature became increasingly concerned about the future of Maine's forests because of the speed with which the region's pine trees were disappearing as the land entered private hands. Through the end of the nineteenth century, as trains made more of Maine accessible, more land was cleared for agriculture each decade. Even so, farmers struggled against poor conditions to produce pork, wool, cheese, wheat, corn, and potatoes for market.[14] It was lumbering, however, not farming, that remained the leading industry in nineteenth-century Maine. The railroads created readier markets for more remote timber, and the large corporations that had snapped up the state's land in mid-century began harvesting with abandon. State leaders in Augusta worried that if the trees disappeared, the entire state, farmers included, would be in trouble. Legislators wanted the forests to be managed more conservatively, though the trees were distant and on private land.[15]

Farmers, too, worried about the effect of the forest industry on the state, but not primarily because of the disappearance of trees. Wage labor in the forest industry, they believed, was harmful to the farm economy. In 1856, the secretary of the Maine Board of Agriculture surveyed the farmers of the state, asking them to describe the lumber industry's effect on farming. Of those who replied, 80 percent said lumbering was hurting agriculture. One writer exclaimed that lumbering was "death! death!" to farming. Among the reasons farmers gave were the exhaustion of oxen after the winter's work, the loss of manure for the fields, farmers still being in the woods at planting time, and exploitative accounts run up at the company store while farmers lived in the logging camps, negating the benefits of winter wages.[16]

Yet their position was an ambiguous one: many farmers depended on jobs with the timber companies to make ends meet. When labor on the farm was at its low point after the snows fell, timber companies throughout Maine were eager to hire what farmers they could, along with the farmers' oxen, to fell trees and pull them across the snow to the rivers, where they would be transported to mills downstream after the spring thaw.[17]

By the time the farmers told the Board of Agriculture their concerns, the state's pine trees were almost gone and the forest industry was changing.

Old-growth pine had long been a prized tree for lumber, because the wood is versatile, relatively free from knots, and the trunks are large and very tall. Early timber harvesters in Maine took little else. In later years, spruce was also used for lumber, hemlock for coarse lumber, and hemlock bark for tanning. The rot-resistant tamarack (also called hackmatack) was used in shipbuilding, and the odorless fir was used for boxes and butter tubs. In the early years, the harvesting of these and other species had remained relatively light while the focus was on pine, but in the mid-nineteenth century, as the pine supply dwindled, trees of every kind began falling to the saw.[18]

With the arrival of the railroad in the late nineteenth century and the resulting access to distant buyers, these secondary trees became more marketable commodities. Cedar, for example, which had previously been used primarily for shingles, became the most valuable tree in the forest. The fresh-scented wood filled a specialty niche for trunks, and it was used widely for roof beams, fence posts, and, most importantly, railroad ties, since it is uncommonly resistant to insects and rot. Other formerly spurned trees found their uses too: white birch was used to make spools, and all of the hardwoods were used for furniture, tools, and boxes. Unlike early pine harvests, late nineteenth-century harvests stripped the land clean.[19]

The biggest change in the Maine forests, though, came with the rise of the pulp and paper industry. After the Civil War, the lumber industry in the state declined as the pine trees vanished, and companies instead turned to Wisconsin, Minnesota, and Michigan to supply their markets. In addition, the northeastern market for lumber was changing as well, as urban building codes encouraged the use of steel, stone, brick, and concrete in the building of dwellings to avoid fire hazards; wooden packing boxes and barrels were being replaced by lighter weight and cheaper paper board and steel containers; and the shipbuilding industry fell off. New technologies in papermaking, however, provided a market for the smaller spruce and poplar trees that had been left behind by loggers in search of pine. As paper companies shifted from using rags to using wood pulp in their factories, the demand for the smaller trees seemed inexhaustible.[20]

As the paper industry expanded in Maine, three interrelated issues of land

and trees preoccupied Maine residents, the legislature, and the timber industry: fires, hunting rights, and state authority over forested lands. All three issues involved definitions of property rights, and what it meant to own trees became contested. In the early twentieth century, it seemed for a while that the public obligations of forest ownership might supersede narrow private property rights. By the 1930s, however, large timber corporations had succeeded in organizing land management practices in Maine to maximize their control of forest property and minimize the public nature of forest ownership.

As the forest industry shifted away from the harvest of high-grade pine toward more intensive operations involving many species and all sizes of trees, logging became more visible to Maine residents. Many farmers and legislators began to speculate about the proper role of the state government in managing a resource so central to the state's economy. In addition, the remaining trees became newly valuable at the same time that the railroads were bringing more remote lands within easier reach of farmers, hunters, and tourists. New waves of tourists and hunters with access to more remote lands presented their own particular threats to the woods with their campfires and their guns. Owners of forested land and state policy makers became increasingly concerned with fire danger, and began searching for ways to protect the newly threatened trees.

As early as 1869, the Maine Board of Agriculture petitioned the state legislature to pass laws "encouraging the preservation and production of forest trees."[21] In language echoing George Perkins Marsh's 1864 *Man and Nature*, Board of Agriculture commissioners Calvin Chamberlain and S. L. Goodale blamed a decline of population centers in Asia, Africa, and southern Europe on "the gradual waste of natural forests" and "a corresponding change in climate."[22] The commissioners warned: "The decay of these once rich and flourishing countries, is mainly the result of man's ignorant disregard for the laws of nature." Maine residents, they argued, faced the same risk: "We are destined soon to be startled by the unpleasant fact that a famine for wood is upon us, unless immediate measures are adopted whereby the supply may be increased, and the destruction of what remains diminished."[23] They were successful in their petition, and in 1869 the Maine legislature passed "An Act for the encouragement of the growth of forest trees." The new law provided tax exemptions for cleared farmland that was replanted in trees.[24]

Yet in contrast to neighboring states, cleared agricultural land was not where forest policy was most important in Maine. By the end of the nineteenth century, ownership of the vast majority of land was concentrated in the hands of just a few companies. The largest two—International Paper and the Great Northern Paper Company—were created in the 1890s through mergers of a number of smaller firms. International Paper's first annual report announced that by way of such mergers, the company controlled 90 percent of the newsprint supply in the East and that "competition was not of a serious nature."[25]

As corporate landholdings were being consolidated, the large landholders turned to the state legislature for help in protecting their property from trespass, fire, and theft. The first substantial steps toward regulating forest use were taken in 1883, when the state legislature passed stricter hunting laws limiting the months in which game could be killed and outlawing all hunting on Sundays. The new laws had been championed by the largest landowners as a way of restricting access to land and monitoring who traveled where and why, thereby cutting down on the frequency of wildfires.[26]

Owning land in the far north, away from towns and transportation networks, was a huge risk. The forests on such land were extremely valuable, but they were also extremely difficult to protect. There was little that absentee landowners or the state could do, for example, to stop people from harvesting timber on land they did not own. Upon traversing their property, large landowners often found that people had not only cut down acres of trees, but also had begun growing wheat in their place. As the illegal cutting of trees, clearing of land, and growing of crops increased and as railroad lines expanded farther into these remote woodlands, there were ever more potential sources of spark and flame. A valuable tract of timberland could be reduced to a fire-scarred field overnight.[27]

Tourists presented corporate landowners in Maine with a huge fire risk. Careless hunters, in particular, could (and did) easily start out-of-control forest fires with sparks from their guns and with campfires. In an effort to reduce

4.5 "Seven and One Hanging—Team in the Woods for More
[detail]." The 1903 haul of a group of hunters in northern Maine: seven
deer and one moose, with more to come. Robert N. Dennis Collection
of Stereoscopic Views, Miriam and Ira D. Wallach Division of Art,
Prints and Photographs, New York Public Library, Astor, Lenox and
Tilden Foundations.

the risk of such fires by reducing unsupervised access to their land (eliminat-
ing access was all but impossible), the largest timber companies offered leases
to hunting camp operators. In 1904, for example, the Great Northern Paper
Company, worried about the unsupervised hunters wandering their property
near Pierce Pond, offered a free lease to their employee Charles Spalding if
he would establish a camp there.[28] It was camps like Spalding's—and others
at Rangeley Lake, Loon Lake, and elsewhere around the state—that were the
focus of the sensational promotions that "Fly Rod" Crosby and her colleagues
put forward at the exhibitions in New York.[29]

The camps were usually located on a river or lake and consisted of a central dining lodge surrounded by smaller cabins. The hope was that inexperienced hunters would use these camps instead of setting off into the woods on their own. Led by well-trained guides who were aware of and prepared for the fire risks, they would be less likely to leave burned-over acreage in their wake. The new game laws were part of the same strategy: the timberland owners hoped that by restricting access to their land to the damp Maine fall, fewer fires would catch and spread. In addition, the new laws favored the hunting camps: out-of-state hunters could count on their guides knowing the rules and planning expeditions accordingly.[30]

Naturalist and folklorist Fannie Pearson Hardy made a point of what she and many others saw as the unfairness of the new laws in a series of columns she wrote for *Forest and Stream* magazine in the early 1890s. She detailed a trip she took into the backwoods of Maine with her father, Manly Hardy, when she was twenty-three years old. The elder Hardy was the guide for the trip, and a hired hand, Jot Eldridge, did most of the cooking and heavy lifting.[31] Hardy catalogued the plants and animals they encountered, and she studied the people they met. She would make her fame in later years with projects she began that fall, collecting folk songs of the Maine woods and documenting Maine's birds.[32] But it was the new hunting rules that most captured her attention. She was angered by what she saw as the discrimination inherent in the laws.

Hardy, her father, and the Maine woodsmen they met on their trip shared a conviction that Maine's new game laws were written to benefit out-of-state hunters and large landowners at the expense of local people. Hardy argued that hunting seasons and bag limits were severely restricted in order to keep locals out of the woods and to guarantee quarry for out-of-state hunters during peak seasons. At the heart of the issue was the premise of the new laws: that the people of Maine did not own the state's game in common, but rather that the animals were property of the state. Ownership of and access to game was intimately tied to control of land and trees. Fannie Hardy and her allies argued that the state was safeguarding the timber industry's interests at the expense of the hunters and farmers. At their core, the laws were about access to land. Corporate owners wanted to keep down the risks of fire, and they also wanted the power to control who used their property. The new laws expanded their ability to exercise such control.[33]

Before the passage of the 1883 game laws, wildlife in Maine had been common property. No one owned the deer or the moose or the partridges, every hunter had as much right to the game as the next, and no one had the right to restrict another's access to the animals, even on private land. Once killed, game became private property; the dead animal belonged to the person who had fired the fatal shot. The game laws, however, transformed this common and private property into public property. After 1883, the animals belonged not to every resident in common, but to the state, and the state of Maine could and did restrict and regulate access to its game.[34]

If an animal was killed or captured when the state said it was illegal to do so, it remained public property and was subject to seizure by the state. The state's assertion of ownership of game, even when that game might be walking across privately owned land or had already been converted from animal to meat, was understood by many Maine residents as a constriction of their property rights. And Maine hunters who depended on game to supplement their diets during harsh northern winters saw outlawing winter hunting as cruel and unfair. The game laws seemed to be designed to cater to the wealthy out-of-staters who came north to hunt for a few weeks out of the year and to the timber corporations that wanted to exclude most people from their lands.[35]

Game has always been a tricky form of property, because it doesn't stay put. Is a deer common property if it is walking across private land? Can it be justifiably publicly regulated on private land? Many late nineteenth-century hunters in Maine said yes to the first question and no to the second. In a state with almost no public land, trespass prohibitions could have kept many people from being able to hunt in Maine at all. In practical terms, however, such prohibitions were impossible. Many of the state's largest landholdings were too vast and too remote for owners to effectively keep hunters out. In contrast, a game warden who could arrest a hunter on the way home for mere possession of a deer out of season could be more effective (and thus more objectionable) in controlling access to land and animals.[36]

When Hardy wrote her *Forest and Stream* columns in 1891, her chief target was state control of property—both land and game. For Hardy, and for the woodsmen she and her father visited with during their northern treks, state control equaled loss of property. For large landowners, however, some state regulation was a small price to pay for safeguarding vast wealth, and they continued to lobby for even stricter game laws. The laws seemed to expand rather than contract their property rights, allowing them to more easily exclude people from their land.[37]

And yet as landowners attempted to define their rights through the courts and through the legislature, restricting access to their land to the fullest extent possible, Maine hunters and farmers (often the same people) resisted. Hardy explained that strict game and trespass laws, though intended to reduce fire risk, in fact might do the opposite. In writing about one strategy used by some landowners—the establishment of game preserves, to which only guests were permitted access—she warned that those excluded might exact what they saw as justice in rather direct form: "Now the punishment of some sins is reserved for God alone, but (according to the Maine dictum) stinginess may be punished by God and the neighbors. There is not the slightest doubt that the establishment of preserves, or even the purchasing of land for them at the present time, would result in burning the country."[38] Landowners, Hardy warned, shouldn't be surprised if game preserves were set afire. Fires were not merely a random risk; they could be political protest, too.

When Cyrus A. Packard became Maine's first forest commissioner in 1891, his primary mandate was to protect forests from fire, and he was somewhat baffled by the task. With the forestry profession in its infancy, and Packard's background as the state land agent offering him little preparation, Packard found himself flailing. Although a forest commission had already been created in nearby New Hampshire and state bureaus had begun forestry work in Pennsylvania and Vermont, none were as focused on firefighting as the commission in Maine. Packard presented his first report "with considerable embarrassment," explaining that "the work was entirely new in this State and nearly so all over the United States." He had turned to other state foresters for advice, but they had had little to offer since "it was not in many instances in other states the *great* object to protect growing timber." In other states, fire protection was secondary to reforestation schemes. Maine was unique because there were still so many trees to protect.[39]

Forest Commissioner Packard's enumeration of the causes of fires revealed the distrust large landowners felt toward their less well-to-do neighbors and unruly passers-through. He reported that 25 percent of fires were caused by "fishermen, sportsmen or tourists," and another 25 percent "by clearing land or burning brush piles." The frequency of land-clearing fires, the commissioner went on to explain, "accounts for the unwillingness of holders of timber lands to sell farm lots." Having farmers as neighbors was just as bad as having unregulated hunters on the land—they used fire and were therefore a risk. Another 10 percent of forest fires, according to the commissioner, were "set to burn over the forest to facilitate the growth of blueberries, or food for deer, or from a desire to destroy property, perhaps for revenge." Packard's implication was clear: the fires were set by irresponsible, lower-class people who had little regard for the property of others. The cause of the remaining 35 percent of fires was reported as "unknown." Fires caused by railroads, mills, and lumbering operations, though they surfaced elsewhere, even in Packard's own report, did not make it into this official list. Unruly lower-class individuals, not organized, responsible corporations, were deemed to be at fault for the fires.[40]

Unlike forest officials in New Hampshire and Vermont, those in Maine saw locals and tourists alike as a threat to forests rather than a help. In New Hampshire and Vermont, both tourists and farmers were integral components of forest management plans. Promoting tourism was seen as a way both to help local farmers survive in a changing economy and to promote tree planting and forest preservation. Without the tourists, both forests and farms would be lost, and vice versa. Tourists to these areas wanted forested vistas as part of

4.6 "Forester's Camp." George S. Kephart Photo Album ("Touring the Maine Woods" August 7-11, 1922), photo 1. Courtesy of the Forest History Society.

4.7 "Foresters at Play." George S. Kephart Photo Album ("Touring the Maine Woods" August 7-11, 1922), photo 2. Courtesy of the Forest History Society.

their vacation landscape, and local people planted and protected and created forested landscapes in part to provide visitors from the city with their imagined country idyll. In Maine, landowners feared that the tourists would burn down the trees.

Forestland owners in Maine were even more terrified by fire after a disastrous run of blazes in 1903, 1905, and 1909, which destroyed over six million dollars in timber and property in 1903 alone. Packard and his successors had conducted active education campaigns to reduce fire risks, but one poorly controlled backcountry campfire could still burn through thousands of dollars of timber before it was even noticed, much less extinguished. What was needed was an organized system of patrols and lookouts to catch fires before they got out of hand.[41]

Beginning in 1903, the Forest Commission hired fire wardens, who patrolled high-risk areas, sometimes carrying buckets of water with them. Only ten thousand dollars in emergency money had been allocated to pay for the patrols, however, so coverage was spotty. Just as the large timber owners had welcomed the regulation of game on their lands, they welcomed the fire patrols as well, only faulting the state for not providing more.[42]

In order to make more effective fire patrolling possible, leaders of the large timber companies banded together to voluntarily tax themselves to provide extra funding to the commissioner's office for the purpose of hiring more fire wardens. The wardens would then patrol the wildlands of the owners who chose to be taxed. The first year it was created, the Maine Forestry District provided Forest Commissioner Edgar E. Ring with an extra fifty thousand dollars. The patrols were so successful that in 1913 the legislature allowed incorporated areas (that is, not only areas designated as wildlands) to join the district, and many did so.[43] The Maine Forestry District assessment didn't seem like a tax to industry owners; rather, it was an investment. The voluntary tax and the resulting increased patrols gave the landowners more control over their land and a more secure financial interest in their trees.

Control of property continued to be severely contested in early twentieth-century Maine, even after the large landowners had secured game laws and fire patrols from the state. Maine residents, landowners, corporate leaders, and government officials clashed repeatedly over the proper uses of and restrictions on private and public property throughout the state, and nowhere was the confusion and disagreement played out so vividly as in struggles over the proper uses of trees growing on what little public land the state still held.

The story of Olive Cousins illustrates how complicated defining public property and private rights can be. In the same years that "Fly Rod" Crosby was traveling the region drumming up business for Maine hunting camps, and Fannie Hardy was penning anti-tourist, anti-game-law screeds, Cousins was staking a different kind of claim in trees, and her neighbors desperately wanted her to lose.

In 1903, the tax assessors of E Plantation in Aroostook County, Maine, began petitioning the state forest commissioner for help in running Cousins out of town. Olive Cousins had been living on state-owned land in the municipality for over a decade, raising her four sons alone while her husband was away in a mental institution. The tax assessors were the only public officials of E Plantation, and they were scandalized by the fact that Cousins frequently entertained male visitors in her small woods cabin. Worst of all, she had given birth to two more sons while her husband was gone. She and the six boys were paupers, and the state was supporting them by allowing them to live on public land and harvest public lumber. "We the assessors as well as the majority of the people do object and kindly await your counsel," the assessors wrote. "She isn't a decent woman and we want to get rid of her."[44]

Cousins didn't want to move, and in her polite letters to the forest commissioner, she explained that while her husband was in the asylum and her children were young, she was dependent on the state for her home. If the state would not support her, she had nowhere else to turn. She complained that the people of E Plantation "do all they can to hurt me, but I have a right to a home as well as any of the rest of them. Here, the rest of the women have a husband to furnish them with homes and I have not. . . . The people on E want to live themselves but they don't want to see anyone else live." She convinced Commissioner Edgar E. Ring that she was a worthy recipient of state aid, and he allowed her to continue living on the state land and to harvest the occasional tree.[45]

4.8   A dramatic northern log drive in mid-twentieth-century Maine. Forest History Society Image Collection Folder "Logging—Log Drives, Logs in River," FHS4981. Courtesy of the Forest History Society.

4.9   Approximately 34 acres of logs and pulpwood (about 9 million board feet) floating downstream in Maine, 1945. Forest History Society Image Collection Folder "Logging—Log Drives, Logs in River," FHS4993. Photograph by Fred J. Shulley for the U.S. Forest Service. Courtesy of the Forest History Society.

Unlike her opponents, whose correspondence was hastily scrawled on plain paper and rife with misspellings and grammatical errors, Cousins's letters were well written and composed, and neatly presented on fancy stationary with floral designs. Her spelling, grammar, and writing paper all implied a higher level of education and privilege than the people who were trying to get rid of her. She was confident, too, that the forest commissioner would understand that she was a better woman than the assessors were men. Assessor McGray, she wrote, "is a nobody, for if he was, he would not try to make a disturbance with a woman that was trying to get along, and he is poor as

Job's turkey himself." She knew all about "Ed McGray's pedigree," she wrote, and it wasn't good.[46]

The plantation assessors continued their protests for years, to no avail. They wanted the land for hunting cabins, storage sheds, lumber income, a post office, a public school—for anything, really, other than supporting Olive Cousins and people like her. Each year brought a new plan, a new public use that would certainly, they hoped, be a better public use. They were never able to get rid of Cousins, but their repeated attempts brought to light fundamental disagreements about public land and state authority. Ultimately, the assessors were not able to keep the state from using the land to support the poor. But because the municipality was so far from the capital in Augusta and because the state's resources for enforcement were so meager, locals often took matters in their own hands. They couldn't run Olive off of the land, but they could cut down her trees.[47]

Part of the difficulty in knowing what to do with public land in E Plantation had to do with the state's curious municipal structure. A plantation in early twentieth-century Maine was an awkward and middling municipality, not quite a town and yet with the potential to become a town. That potential created an odd conundrum for land management. When Maine separated from Massachusetts in 1820, the entire region had been surveyed and divided into six-mile-square townships. If at least two hundred people lived in the township and if the residents so desired, they could incorporate as a town. Incorporated towns had numerous rights and responsibilities, including the right to own and purchase land and the obligation to support paupers living within the town limits. One of the benefits of incorporating as a town was that the state granted each town four public lots of 320 acres each. One lot was to be for the support of the first minister to settle in the town, one was to support his ministry, one was to support the public schools, and one was the town's to do with as it pleased.[48]

The residents of a township with two hundred people or more might choose not to incorporate as a town, but they were obligated to at least incorporate as a plantation for the purpose of collecting state taxes. Plantations had fewer privileges than towns but also fewer obligations. Plantations, for example, could not own land or incur debts; yet neither were they obligated to support paupers living within their borders.

Plantations could, and often did, become towns. Therefore, though plantations had neither the privilege nor the duty of managing public lots, those lots had to be set aside to assure that they would be available if the plantation later became a town. Often one of the most difficult parts of incorporating as a plantation or as a town was designating public lots. If the incorporation came too late in the settlement of a township, it was possible that all of the land would already have been distributed and settled, requiring the acquisition of public lots through eminent domain.[49]

Once public lots had been identified and set aside within a plantation, the land was managed by the state forest commissioner with the goal of preserving the value in the land for the future benefit of the town. In the meantime, the state could rent out the lots for hunting camps, harvest some of the timber for sale, or allow people to temporarily settle on the land. The income from the lots was to be used to support the plantation's schools, to support paupers within the plantation, or in some other manner for the benefit of the plantation. The forest commissioner worked out the particulars of the management plan with the plantation's only officials, the assessors. Each plantation had three assessors who performed the limited corporate functions of the municipality.[50]

People had many designs on the public lands in the plantations, which were referred to collectively as the "school lots" or "blocks." Some assumed that public land was common land and public timber common timber and acted accordingly. They would cut small amounts of wood from the school lots for fuel and for repairing farm buildings, and they would camp and hunt on the land. Other people went further, cutting trees to sell to lumber mills and paper companies. Still others erected homes or hunting cabins. The state forest commissioner tried, through the intermediaries of the plantation assessors, to regulate the uses to which the school lots were put and to exact fees for their use, but there were frequent obstacles.

Plantation residents considered the land to be theirs in common, even though it was legally state land. Unlike town residents, they had no direct legal control of the land, but they felt strongly that they should be able to decide who had legitimate claims on the local public resources. In E Plantation in particular, many people believed that Olive Cousins—because of her poverty and loose morals—had no legitimate claim on resources that should rightly benefit the municipality as a whole. The residents of E Plantation had chosen to incorporate as a plantation instead of a town precisely to avoid having to support people like Cousins. They saw it as outrageously unfair to be forced by the state to accommodate her when there were so many better uses for *their* public land.

In the early years of the twentieth century, the forest commissioner was able to pay regular visits to the plantations near Augusta. When disagreements arose over the proper management plans for the public lots or over the precise location of the lots' boundaries, the commissioner surveyed the area before rendering a decision on the proper use of the land and the trees. For more remote plantations, he had to rely on letters from the plantation assessors and plantation residents to inform him about the condition of the land and trees. Often, the forest commissioner would receive contradictory reports from local people with different interests in the land and property.[51] Both the commissioner and many local people were frustrated by the state's inability to make informed decisions or to enforce decisions once they were made. For others, the remoteness of state authority worked in their favor.[52]

When the forest commissioner granted a person permission to use a school lot, others in the plantation often argued that they should be able to enjoy the same privilege. For example, when Irwin Sprague was given permission to build a hunting cabin on a public lot in Plantation 21 in Washington County, his neighbor Lewis Crosby strenuously objected. Officially, Sprague's application was successful because he had promised not to cut any timber, was willing to pay a five dollar annual fee to lease the land, and the assessors of Plantation 21 had vouched for his character and for the suitability of a hunting cabin on the lot. In his positive response to Sprague's request, the commissioner explained that "[w]e have many applications for just such privileges, but only in a few instances have we granted any such right." Lewis Crosby thought he understood precisely why Sprague was favored. "I can pay five dollars as well as Sprague, but I am not a Granger[,] nothing to[o] good for them," he wrote. Sprague and the assessors were members of the same political organization, and so he was able to make uses of public lands that others could not. "The poor people who paid taxes to git the Blocks have no chance with you and two of the assessors," Crosby complained.[55]

Even when the forest commissioner actively tried to avoid cronyism, the plantation assessors and their friends and families found ways to get what they wanted. On Caswell Plantation, for example, when the commissioner would not grant plantation assessor Noah Berube permission to log on the public lots, Berube simply got his mother to apply for a permit. Eugia Berube received the permit with ease.[56]

When the forest commissioner denied logging permits on remote public lots in an attempt to manage the land for future timber revenues, he often lost both the current and future value of the timber. Those who had been denied permits faced few, if any, repercussions if they cut the wood they wanted anyway. In 1903, an assessor of Caswell Plantation wrote to Commissioner Ring to point out to him the futility of denying logging permits: "I will say that I do not like to interfere with anyone's business. But I do not like to see things going that way. Now I been send you for permit to cut on the public lot for these last 3 yrs. And you wouldn't give the permissions to cut any thing. And now them same men that come to me to write you for a permit and when they see that you would not give any permit they say now if we cannot git any permit we're going to steal some, and it has been that way since I can remember. So now you can see in to it your self, and do what you like about it. I would like to cut a few logs this fall and I don't like to steal them. But if I don't, probably that some one else would before long."[57] The assessor encouraged the commissioner to just accept the fact that trees would be cut and take advantage of the fact that people were willing to pay small fees for permits to do it legally.

The commissioner met the fiercest opposition if he attempted to use the land or the lumber to meet the state obligation to support the paupers of a plantation. Local officials believed that public land ought to be used to benefit the public, and making it possible for paupers to stay in the area was far from a public benefit. It was a nuisance. The assessors of E Plantation argued repeatedly that the greater public good would be better served by getting Olive Cousins to just go away. Assessor Robert Hafford wrote to Commissioner Ring that Cousins's house was a "horehouse," and "it would be a god blasen to the plantation if she was of[f] it."[58]

When the assessors of E Plantation couldn't get rid of Olive, they cut down the trees near her house. Cousins complained to the forest commissioner when one of the assessors cut one hundred dollars worth of what she considered her timber and told her that he was going to cut more; when the commissioner was unable to put a stop to the harvesting, she let him know that she was going to increase her harvest as well. But when she brought her logs to the mill to be cut into railroad ties for sale, the town assessors confiscated them and notified the forest commissioner that she was stealing wood. In her frustration, Olive Cousins began petitioning the forest commissioner to allow her to purchase the land on which she lived so that her rights could not be constantly challenged. But the land was not the state's to sell; it had to be held in trust for a possible future town.[59]

The end of Olive Cousins's story remains unclear, since the records of correspondence between the residents of E Plantation and the forest commissioner come to an abrupt end in 1912. Perhaps the correspondence stopped, or, more likely, record-keeping practices changed. But her struggles with her neighbors and the authorities of the state highlight the degree to which popular understandings of the proper uses and meanings of public property were up for debate.

The experiences of Cousins, Berube, and Lewis Crosby illustrate that just as the timber companies were consolidating control over their forestland, the state was functionally unable to manage the land it owned. Timber companies, with their highly organized and well-compensated advocates lobbying for them in Augusta, were able to make a strong case that corporate-owned forestland was more efficiently managed than that owned by the state. By doing so, they effectively blocked several legislative efforts to create large publicly owned forests in Maine. In the years between the land sales of the 1860s and the end of the twentieth century, less than 3 percent of Maine was in public hands. This is in sharp contrast to the rest of the Northeast, where public land acquisition played a much larger role in reforestation. Almost all of Maine's forests, old and new, are on private land.[60]

That has meant, among other things, that Maine is for sale. Between 1998 and 2004, over a third of the land in Maine—more than seven million acres—changed hands. And in changing hands, the character of the land-holding has changed as well. Forests in Maine had been concentrated among relatively few owners and were often managed somewhat conservatively for a sustained timber harvest. Both timber corporations and individuals like Cousins and her neighbors had an interest in the future of trees. Though privately held, the large tracts were often available to hunters like Hardy and guides like "Fly Rod" Crosby, because their carefully managed presence helped the owners keep tabs on their property. But as the timber industry has become both global and fragmented, fewer companies are managing for generational stability. Instead of vertically integrated companies owning vast acres for decades on end, moving from one harvest-ready stand to the next as its mills are ready for the next shipment of logs, twenty-first century corpora-tions now specialize—the land, the trees, and the factories are often owned by different entities, in different parts of the world. When a plot of forestland changes hands in Maine, it is often immediately shorn of its trees and then sold again to a vacation-home developer or other speculator.

There have been some recent efforts to slow the shifts in land use. In 1970, the Maine State Legislature established the Land Use Regulation Commis-sion (LURC) to manage lands outside of organized cities and towns, and the commission's purview has expanded over the years. In 1989, the state passed the Forest Practices Act to regulate timber-harvesting methods, and recent land purchases by Maine's Department of Conservation finally brought pub-lic land holdings in the state above a still-meager 5 percent. Yet Maine's for-ests remain in real danger, in ways that contrast with those of other states in the region. Maine's woods are being cut at an alarming rate, and new owners continue to rapidly convert the former timber tracts to other uses.[61]

Without the tax policies, public holdings, and municipal controls put in place elsewhere in the Northeast in the first years of the twentieth century, the forests there would be in danger just as grave. Yet those forests, while more protected, are not without risk, and resource managers in those states would do well to look to Maine as a warning of the potential dangers of thinking of forests in isolation. Forests elsewhere in the region were well integrated into landscapes and regulation schemes that included cities, farms, wildlands, habitat, and timber; in Maine, forests were managed as merely trees, which means that many more of them are coming down.

"Fly Rod" Crosby, Fannie Hardy, and Olive Cousins, each in her own way, worked hard to craft public spaces and secure public rights in the Maine woods. Despite working for different publics and seeing different uses and values in the forests and trees, each woman argued strenuously for a public interest in the woods. But their voices are being lost, along with the trees they depended on. That loss is in part because the reach of the region's cities did not quite make it to the northern woods of Maine. And that is unfortunate, because today the woods of Maine—and the woods of the entire Northeast, and the world—are more closely connected to urban people and urban places than ever before. The dependencies between cities and forests have never been more crucial or more clear.

4.10   Interior of a mesophytic *Picea* [spruce] forest, Mt. Katahdin, Maine. University of Chicago Library, Special Collections Research Center, Department of Botany Records, mep54.

CHAPTER FIVE

Fractured Forests and the Future of Northeastern Trees

I n July 2009, a black bear snacked on a pet rabbit in Passaic County, New Jersey. "The bear was just sauntering down the street," said Luiz Katz, who saw the bear loping through the neighborhood before it crushed an outdoor rabbit cage, scooped up the pet, and headed back into the woods.[1] This is now normal: black bears live in suburban New Jersey, along with growing herds of deer, packs of coyotes, rafters of wild turkeys, and the occasional gray fox.

A couple of months after the rabbit snack incident, a three-hundred-pound mama bear and her cub were spotted in suburban Trenton, prompting state senators to demand that Governor Jon Corzine authorize a bear hunt in the state. Republican senators issued a press release about the bear: "This is a wild animal," they announced. "It didn't just fall off a circus train."[2] No hunt was allowed. The bear and her cub may not have fallen off a circus train, but neither were they out of place. New Jersey, as John McPhee put it almost three decades ago, has become "a textbook place for bears."[3] When McPhee was describing New Jersey as ideal bear habitat in the early 1980s, there were fewer than two dozen documented bears in the state. By 1992 there were so many that newspapers were reporting sightings at the Paramus Mall. By the

5.1 A Pennsylvania bear looking for directions (or perhaps just snacks). U.S. Forest Service Region 9, photograph R9_343871. Courtesy of the Forest History Society.

end of the first decade of the twenty-first century, bears were living in every county in the state, and the population was thousands strong.[4]

A week after the mama bear and her cub wandered through Trenton, a black bear strolled by the Old Rustic Mall in downtown Manville, New Jersey. He crossed the railroad tracks and made his way across a few lawns while the local police called for help. Then the bear just wandered away. A local paper quoted a spokesperson for the state Department of Environmental Protection, who explained that the sighting was not a rare event or even cause for concern: "Black bears are a part of the natural landscape, so sightings are not a problem," said Darlene Yuhas.[5]

Malls, trees, cars, pet rabbits, and roving carnivores are all part of the twenty-first-century northeastern landscape, one in which the boundaries between city and hinterland are not nearly so stark as some would imagine or wish them to be. Sprawling suburbs have become part of the sprawling woods, with corridors of wildness connecting city and forest, sometimes seeming to threaten both.

Herbert Welsh would have had something in common with these twenty-first-century bears. On his long walks from Pennsylvania to New Hampshire, he—like the bears—experienced the region as a single connected place. It has only been in recent years that people have come to see boundaries between the region's wild nature and tamed human habitat as necessary or even possible to police. This new insistence on keeping nature in its place is in part because the nonurban spaces of the Northeast now seem so much more wild. When Christopher Wren set out on his long walk from Times Square to Vermont, he had to be far more careful of wild animals than did Welsh.

Northeastern forests in the early twenty-first century are robust. They are thick with creatures, plant life, and rich habitats that seem very far removed from the neighboring cities that have nurtured them. The forests serve the burgeoning populations of the northeastern corridor with clean water, space to play, timber products, and beautiful views. They offer vacation space for hikers and hunters from throughout the region, jobs for many in the leisure and resource industries, and habitats for animals large and small. The woods, the cities, and the sprawl in between have become ever more visibly intertwined.

Such extensive woods are only possible because of the region's connections with and dependence on agricultural and industrial landscapes in distant places. If it were not for grain from the Midwest, fruit from the West and the South, meat from around the world, and lumber from distant woods, these trees would long ago have been felled for timber, cleared for other uses of land, or both.

The forests of the Northeast are not the same as they were three hundred, or five hundred, or a thousand years ago. They are neither precontact forests nor pristine woods; while wild, they are new and young, and with different and often impoverished mixtures of trees and other plant and animal life.

Many of the new trees are small, and most of the new forests are fractured. Roads wind among the trees, houses are scattered through the groves, and ski trails are carved into forested hills.

Though young, fractured, and dependent, these forests are critical components of northeastern ecosystems and worthy of both respect and protection. The region is far richer for its trees: they protect drinking water, moderate flood and drought, and provide shade, beauty, and habitat and a measure of timber and wood, even at their most scraggly, unmanaged, and thin. But without care and foresight—well grounded in the history that has brought the forests back—those hard-won riches could very easily be lost.

As the stories from Pennsylvania, New Hampshire, Vermont, and Maine have shown, the roads to forest protection will vary among the states. One of environmental history's most important contributions to our understanding of the past has been to push us away from the narrative and analytical constraints imposed by the conventions of political boundaries, and it is that perspective that allows us to see cities and their hinterlands, near and far, as part of intertwined and dependent spaces. Sometimes political boundaries matter, but in environmental stories, they often distract from other bounds: the significant unit of analysis is often not the state, but rather the forest, the watershed, or the river, all of which may cross multiple state lines. In taking politics out of the center of stories and putting nature there, environmental historians have opened up new ways of looking at the past. This insight is true and of great value in understanding the connections between, for example, forests in New Hampshire and cities in Massachusetts. Yet state resource policies and tax codes, state tourist boards and water management regimes, state municipal structures: these all shape the possibilities for protecting and managing the Northeast's new twenty-first-century forests.

Political boundaries matter. Ecological boundaries are rarely independent of political arrangements, as politics, taxes, and municipal structures affect the shape of the land. The history of northeastern reforestation demonstrates the influence that state agencies, commissions, and fiscal policies have on land-use patterns and on decisions whether to plant or cut trees. The forests have returned to the many states in different ways and must be protected in different ways as well. More public ownership of woodlands is almost certainly necessary in Maine, while stronger forest-friendly agricultural policy is likely the better way forward in Vermont. In Massachusetts, forward-thinking foresters and land-use planners are working with a combination of those paths.

Most important in each case is to keep at the center of forest management policy the central truth that forests and cities—within states, across state lines, and around the world—are intertwined ecosystems and must be thought about and managed together. When a bear shows up in the sprawling parking lot of New Jersey's Paramus Mall, when a wild turkey sprints through Boston, when a coyote skips through the Holland Tunnel into TriBeCa for the afternoon, it is clear that boundaries between wild nature and urban centers are fictions. And even the fictions, like the trees, are new.

One town center in particular forcefully drives this point home. Moose and eagles are common sights in Dana, in central Massachusetts, and bears and coyotes traipse through at will. But unlike in forested towns elsewhere in the Northeast, there are no local people in Dana to be disturbed. This town in the Swift River Valley, seventy-five miles from Boston, was dismantled in 1938. Houses were torn down and bodies were dug up from the graveyard. The church, the school, and the town hall were stripped to their foundations, which now peek through the woods. Dana, along with the towns of Prescott, Enfield, and Greenwich, was emptied of people—living and dead—to prepare for the flooding of the Swift River behind the Winsor Dam. The resulting thirty-nine-square-mile Quabbin Reservoir has provided drinking water for Boston ever since, and the fifty-six thousand acres of now open space surrounding the Quabbin provide both protection for the water supply and some of the best wildlife habitat in the state.[6]

The town green at Dana is a spooky relic in the woods, a more stark and dramatic echo of the stone walls and cellar holes that hikers frequently stumble across in the forests of the Northeast. At Dana, a lot more is visible than the low walls that used to line the edges of fields. The edges of the town common are still legible in the remnants of buildings and roads that hugged it almost a century ago. Foundations of civic buildings and homes are still visible, and granite headstones still mark graves that once held bodies long since disinterred and reburied outside of the reservoir catchment zone. The Metropolitan District Commission—the state agency tasked with managing the Boston water supply—even keeps the old roads plowed. At Dana, emptied to create a forest buffer for the Quabbin Reservoir, the multiple levels of the history of northeastern reforestation have become particularly visible and so easily read on the land.

At first glance, the new wilderness seems accidental. One historian of the reservoir and its surroundings embraces that thought in his book title. Thomas Connuel's *Quabbin: The Accidental Wilderness* tells of the unexpected benefits to wildlife that came with the flooding of the Swift. And yet the eighty-year-old forest of maple, oak, and birch is no accident; it is the result of decades of careful planning, of strategic public purchases, and the purposeful unbuilding of towns and relocation of residents both living and dead to create a landscape of water and trees that would flourish in service to a city an hour-and-a-half drive away.[7] The Commonwealth of Massachusetts created the Quabbin wilderness so that Boston and other nearby cities would have clean drinking water for generations to come.

There is a danger in seeing the Quabbin and its sister wildernesses of the region as more natural than they are. Viewing the woods of central Massachusetts, of northern New Jersey, of upstate New York, of western Pennsylvania, even of far-away Maine as merely the result of happenstance does three things: it obscures the importance of the complicated tax and land policy decisions made by northeasterners and their governments in the first years of the twentieth century, allowing the presence of mature trees today to seem inevitable rather than historically contingent; it removes cities from their rightful place at the center of any conservation policy plans for the region; and it masks the Northeast's complicated role in world forest and agricultural politics. Residents of the region are not innocent beneficiaries of accidental re-wilding, but privileged people whose wild environs are possible only because specific decisions have allowed new trees to take firm root at the same time that food and wood products flooded into the Northeast from other environments around the world.

And so it is that Dana and the Quabbin highlight the many scales we must choose among when we try to see the northeastern trees. Do we see the small towns of central Massachusetts, abandoned almost a century ago and now ensconced in woods, highlighting the contrast between human settlements and habitat for bears? Or do we use a slightly wider lens to see the wilderness as an artifact of Boston's need for safe, clean drinking water? Do we step back further still and take in the protected headwaters of the streams that feed the Quabbin, the forests that line their banks, and the hikers who revel in that protected, wild-seeming land? The widest view of all is also crucial: northeastern forests and cities depend on deforested, degraded landscapes far from home. A truly responsible forest policy in the twenty-first century must keep the global perspective in sight. Forest management in Massachusetts—past and present—helps us bring those various scales into conversation with one another, allowing us to see their overlapping and sometimes contradictory truths.

Like Philadelphia, Harrisburg, Pittsburgh, New York, New Haven, Providence, and dozens of smaller cities throughout the Northeast, Boston's booming mid-nineteenth-century growth sent city leaders to the hinterland in search of dependable and pure supplies of water. In the late nineteenth century, they turned to the watershed of the Sudbury River, but could see early on that the supplies those waters provided would not be sufficient over the long term.

Construction of the Quabbin began in 1927, shortly after the state appropriated sixty-five million dollars to clear the valley and impound its river. About 2,500 living residents were displaced, and even more of the dead: 7,500 graves were moved to make way for city water and the buffer of woods that would protect it. Now, 2.5 million people depend on the 412 billion gallons of unfiltered water that the Swift River Valley can contain.[8]

So far, because of early action to create buffers and impose development restrictions within the reservoir watershed, Boston—like New York—has been able to avoid building the water filtration plants that so many cities—Philadelphia among them—have come to depend on. Philadelphia built its water system too early and too close to the city and has had to filter its water for over a century. But New York and Boston have reservoirs deeply enough ensconced in woods that those cities have escaped the billion-dollar costs of building and maintaining filtration plants.⁹

As the twentieth century drew to a close, the U.S. Environmental Protection Agency began questioning the wisdom of allowing the largest water supply systems in the country to remain unfiltered, but to date Boston and New York City have managed to pass all tests (or at a minimum, meet the deadlines for passing tests). It is in large part their material connections and importance to the city that keep so many acres in western Massachusetts and upstate New York in trees.¹⁰

In the 1990s, when the EPA tried to require New York City to build a $6.5 billion filtration plant, one of the selling points was that filtration technology could ease development restrictions upstate. If the city were to build the plant, property values in the hinterland could rise, but many Catskill locals did not want to see regulation disappear. Family farmers and small woodlot owners began to negotiate with New York City, New York State, and the federal government to preserve the development regulations that had created the landscape from which they made a living. In 1997, they reached an agreement. The city, more than two dozen Catskill communities, the U.S. Environmental Protection Agency, and numerous state agencies and environmental organizations signed a $1.4 billion agreement to avoid the necessity of filtration by further restricting development, improving local sewage and septic systems, and exploring new and more ecologically sensitive agricultural and timber harvesting techniques. Higher city water bills now pay for training programs for loggers and dairy farmers and for the purchase of particularly sensitive tracts of land.¹¹

Not everyone was happy with the agreement. Real estate developers and some property owners objected to the region's development limitations. But many people saw the watershed agreement as a model in which city and hinterland interests converged. One of the program's forest managers, Alan White, pointed to the essence of the agreement: "It is their watershed, but it is our livelihood."¹² In this one case, urban tourism, rural labor, urban water needs, and rural economies have worked together to preserve the Catskills, a forested landscape that is managed, inhabited, fragmented, and new. Despite being neither "natural" nor pristine, these forests are of great value to New York City, New York State, and the Northeast.[13]

Measuring that value, quantifying it for policy makers and constituents, and making it clear just how crucial forests are, not just for bears and coyotes but also for farmers and woodlot owners and city residents, is often a difficult task. In recent years, the concept of "ecosystem services" has come into vogue, and ecologists and planners have been assigning dollar figures to the water filtration services, flood mitigation services, air quality services and the like that forest cover contributes to the Northeast and to ecosystems around the world. For example, the U.S. Forest Service calculated that in 2000, New York State's estimated 253.6 million trees on urban or community land (that is, trees on land identified by the U.S. Census as having settled human communities—a mere 10.8 percent of the state) provided almost $1.5 billion worth of carbon storage, carbon removal, and air pollution removal services alone.[14] The agency puts the number for Massachusetts's 178 million trees on such land that year (about 40.4 percent of the state) at over a billion dollars as well.[15]

Forest cover beyond cities and towns provides greater services still, even if calculating exact dollar figures for such functions can seem absurd. The newly wild land surrounding the Quabbin provides an excellent case in point and is a centerpiece of a visionary plan that has been crafted in Massachusetts in recent years. The *Wildlands and Woodlands* proposal, which has grown out of decades of study at the Harvard Forest, was first formally articulated in a policy paper in 2005, and policy makers following the recommendations in the paper have already secured more and better forest cover for the state and beyond. The plan argues for tax and conservation easement policies to encourage responsible forestry on private lands, and it advocates public purchase of land that ought to be kept wild.[16]

One of its most attractive features is its careful distinction between "wildlands" and "woodlands"—the former intended to be left unmanaged as much as possible, the latter to be responsibly managed for both lumber and other uses. And yet there is an odd blindness to history and human agency in pieces of the document, a history that serves to strengthen the very case the authors intend to advance. The new forests of Massachusetts it seeks to protect are not "an inadvertent consequence of decisions made by thousands of independent individuals," as the proposal makes clear a mere paragraph later, when it celebrates the fact that "fortunately, approximately 20 percent (1 million acres) of Massachusetts is already protected from development."[17] That a fifth of the state is protected land is the result not of the inadvertence of individuals but of the actions of organizations of people and their governments—city, state, and federal—who saw the connections early on between cities and trees.

Wildlands and Woodlands offers insightful and practical ways to build on the achievements of the early twentieth century. But it would be even more useful if it actively drew on that heritage and put the city at the center of the story. The proposal's authors want to add one and a half million more acres to the one million acres of state land already under protection in Massachusetts. That goal is in much closer reach in the context of the history of that first million acres, the legacy of land-use policies that have safeguarded and served farmers, forests, industrialists, wildlife, and city dwellers for over a century.

Forest ecosystems, the proposal makes clear, are of critical value not just to the immediate locale of the trees, and to the general area, and to cities downstream, and to the region as a whole, but also to the globe. As components of young and growing forests, for example, the trees of the Northeast have a voracious appetite for carbon, which means that they absorb more carbon each year than forests elsewhere on the planet—in the Brazilian rain forest, for example—with far older, larger, and therefore slower growing trees.[18]

Such an argument for northeastern forest protection can be dangerous, though, as it can obscure both the history of the northeastern woods and their debt to distant lands. It suggests that northeasterners are doing the planet a kindness by protecting trees at home while consuming wood harvested elsewhere; trees in the Northeast are by no means more worthy of protection than forests far away, even if the relative youth of northeastern trees means less carbon in the planetary atmosphere. It is a wealthy nation's hubris to both produce irresponsible levels of carbon emissions and then argue that forest cover at home, not abroad, should be left standing to help mitigate that fact.

Wildlands and Woodlands suggests no such thing; it specifically proposes less dependence on distant woods and more harvesting of local trees as strategies both for bringing more land under protection and for educating people about the effects of cutting trees and consuming their wood.[19] The carbon sink arguments for valuing the young northeastern woods, however, leave open a problematic rhetorical door: that these new forests provide services that older woods cannot, and that this situation has come about in an accidental way. Such an understanding of the northeastern woods could suggest a complacency about deforestation elsewhere on the globe, alongside a self-righteousness about offsetting carbon emissions at home. But it need not. Northeasterners only have the luxury of imagining their carbon footprint as offset by forest growth because of thinking that divides forest from farm from city. But all are implicated and connected and must be considered in both management plans and accountings of ecosystem services and costs. The authors of *Wildlands and Woodlands* understand this about both the history and the future of the northeastern forests; more of an emphasis on human agency in the past and the many scales of global responsibilities moving into the future will make proposals like this one and policies flowing from them even stronger than they now are.

Forest management plans today must be global, embedded in larger strategies that acknowledge the Northeast as a single place, with wildlands, woodlands, suburbs, and cities: the region's carbon production and carbon absorption go hand in hand. A landowner is not helping the globe by planting an extra acre in trees if she is also using a gasoline-powered snow blower to clear hiking paths through the new woods.

Both wilderness and self-sufficiency are fictions and fetishes: we must be less focused on protecting the pristine and more focused on protecting the earth as a whole. That means more intentional and careful use of forest resources in the Northeast, as well as nurturing the ways the northeastern forests are serving the cities of the region and the ways forests elsewhere are serving both the Northeast and their own local areas. It means seeing cities and their surroundings—large and small, plant and animal, water and asphalt, air and soil—as coherent, dependent systems.

If the Catskills and the Quabbin provide an encouraging story of twenty-first-century forest protection, Harrisburg, Pennsylvania, provides a sobering contrast. If Mira Dock were to find herself at Wetzel's Swamp today, she would be shocked and saddened by what she would see. The park that she and Horace McFarland worked so hard to secure for Harrisburg still exists, but it is surrounded by truck terminals, a community college, and an approach to Interstate 81. The creeks feeding the Susquehanna near Harrisburg are lined with trailer parks and tract homes, highways and shopping malls. The city's drinking water is kept safe not by a sylvan watershed, but by a water treatment plant.[20] Science and urban growth are just as capable of obscuring people's place within ecological systems as they are of nurturing those connections.

The policies of the 1890s to the 1930s have left the Northeast with a legacy not just of trees but also of public lands, nurseries, fire protection plans, favorable tax laws, and forestry schools, organizations, and administrative bodies. Turn-of-the-century forest activists, scientists, politicians, farmers, workers, and tourists shaped the context in which northeastern forests returned, and in which they are managed today. But with the rise of automobile suburbs since World War II and the more recent proliferation of edge cities, the future of forests at the city's doorstep is unclear. The historical moment that linked reforestation with the city's growth may be at an end.

A hundred years ago, hikers like Herbert Welsh, forest activists like Mira Dock, mothers like Olive Cousins, ministers like Everett Hale, hobby farmers like the Oppenheims, and foresters like Philip Ayres understood the connections between city and hinterland, between people and trees, even if they didn't always understand the ways the connections worked. The boundary between urban and wild was created and rarefied in the twentieth-century Northeast in ways that would have been incomprehensible a few generations ago. And while modern-day hikers, like Christopher Wren's companions on the Appalachian Trail, may be baffled by the plausibility of setting out on a hike to Vermont from the wilds of Time Square, nonhuman animals continue to live not just as though urban boundaries are permeable, as of course they are, but also as though they are mere figments of our imagination, which is also true.

5.2 Lucky Pierre (later renamed Otis) being taken out of New York City's Central Park. Douglas Martin, "Wild (and Unleashed) Coyote Is Captured in Central Park," *New York Times*, 2 April 1999, page B1. Photograph by Dith Pran; courtesy of the *New York Times*.

In 1999, when a coyote was captured in Central Park across from the Pierre Hotel, he made the front page of the *New York Times*. "Lucky Pierre" was taken to the Bronx Zoo to be examined and quarantined until he was considered healthy enough to join three compatriots at the Great Plains exhibit of the Queens Wildlife Center. A year later, he happily celebrated his one-year anniversary in Queens, though his name was a source of debate. While some of his defenders and captors remembered him fondly as "Lucky Pierre," others called him "Courtney Coyote." The staff at the Wildlife Center would have none of either; they called their young charge Otis.[21]

A decade later, Otis was still living on display, billed by the Queens Zoo as the "wily survivor" among the captive pack.[22] It seemed for a moment in 2006 that he might get new urban explorer company: Hal the Coyote (so named because he was first sighted near Central Park's Hallett Nature Sanctuary) eluded wildlife officers in Central Park for three days before being captured, quarantined, and tagged. Hal's captors, though, decided a better future for him would be a wildlife refuge in Westchester County. He would never make it: just as a wildlife biologist was tagging his ear in preparation for setting him free, his heart stopped. A *New York Times* obituary for "Hal Coyote, 1, Known For Romp in Central Park," speculated that the stress of his final three days had been too much for him to bear.[23]

Today, coyotes in New York City are no longer strange and are rarely honored with names and biographies in the *New York Times*. The city's park website even lists the animals among "Common New York City Wildlife in Parks," along with peregrine falcons, red-tailed hawks, white-tailed deer, possums, and rats. They are frequent visitors to Brooklyn and the Bronx, and they show up not infrequently in Manhattan as well. As they view bears in suburban New Jersey, wildlife officials now see coyotes not as frightening beasts to be returned to the wild but as among the many wild animals that wander through the landscape and often turn up on the other side of a boundary that only humans discern.[24]

Search-and-capture missions are no longer part of New York City's coyote response, something New Yorkers are sometimes surprised to learn. In March 2010, city officials again were called in to capture a coyote, this time in TriBeCa. Ever since she had been seen scurrying through the Holland Tunnel, she'd been making a home in the neighborhood, and it was two days before officers could find her and move her up to the Bronx. She was the fourth coyote spotted in Manhattan that year, and the first to be captured. Officials likely would not have bothered with her either, but condo owners and commuters kept calling in fear and surprise.[25]

The new forests of the Northeast are home to many beasts that had no place in the region a century ago—and not just in the national forests and state parks but on farm woodlots, behind suburban homes, even on city streets. Wildlife corridors, both accidental and planned, connect Fairmount Park in Philadelphia, Central Park in New York City, and Boston Common not just with the Delaware Water Gap, the Catskills, and the Quabbin but with the woodlands and wild forests of Vermont and New Hampshire, the timberlands and hunting grounds of Maine, and all of the treed acres, corridors, and byways in between. The urban Northeast and the northeastern woods grew up together; they can become impoverished together, but that need not be so. If the connections between city and forest become recognized and nurtured, if we see the cities and woods as the interdependent, uninterrupted landscape that the bears and coyotes know them to be, then we can find ways to protect both. Northeastern cities and trees have flourished together for a hundred years, and both are far richer for it. They should and can nourish each other for the next hundred as well.

5.3 A forester points out the site of the "Once Flourishing Town of Griffith," now part of the Green Mountain National Forest in Vermont. Detail of U.S. Forest Service Region 9, photograph R9_408256. Courtesy of the Forest History Society.

Notes

INTRODUCTION

1. A. J. E., review of *The New Gentleman of the Road*, by Herbert Welsh, *Pennsylvania Magazine of History and Biography* 45 (1921): 396; Herbert Welsh, *The New Gentleman of the Road* (Philadelphia: Wm. F. Fell and Co., Printers, 1921), 13, 31, 39–40, 62, 85, 89, 121; Philip Ayres to Herbert Welsh, June 1925, box 76 (Forestry), folder A-W (1925), Herbert Welsh Collection, Historical Society of Pennsylvania, Philadelphia (hereafter cited as HWC); and Philip Ayres to Herbert Welsh, 17 August 1918 and September 1918, box 75 (Forestry), folder A-W (1918), HWC.

2. Reforestation statistics come from a variety of sources, and are not always gathered or presented in ways that are directly comparable. The statistics in this paragraph come from Thomas J. Considina Jr., *An Analysis of New York's Timber Resources, U.S. Department of Agriculture, for the Forest Service, Northeastern Forest Experiment Station*, Resource Bulletin NE-80 (Washington, D.C.: Government Printing Office, 1984); Christopher McGrory Klyza, "The Northern Forest: Problems, Politics and Alternatives," in *The Future of the Northern Forest*, ed. Christopher McGrory Klyza and Stephen C. Trombulak (Hanover, N.H.: University Press of New England, 1994), 39; Lloyd C. Irland, *Wildlands and Wood-*

lots: The Story of New England's Forests (Hanover, N.H.: University Press of New England, 1982), 2; and U.S. Department of Agriculture, Forest Service, National (FIA) Forest Inventory and Analysis Databases, "Forest Inventory Data Online (FIDO)," http://apps.fs.fed.us/fido (data accessed spring 2001).

Information for the reforestation maps in the following chapters is drawn from publications of the U.S. Forest Service's Northeastern Forest Experiment Station; state forestry commission reports and other publications; the USFS Forest Inventory and Analysis Databases referenced above; and Charles S. Sargent, *Report on the Forests of North America (exclusive of Mexico), Tenth Census of the United States, 1880* (Washington D.C.: Government Printing Office, 1884). For more information on reforestation statistics and also on how the maps were created, see "A Note on the Maps" in the front of this volume. Special thanks are due Rachel Hope Allison for giving visual expression to the changes over time.

The reforestation maps and statistics presented here should be understood as illustrative, not as numerical representations of precise changes, since methods of gathering and expressing information about forest cover have changed dramatically since 1880, when Charles Sargent asked local officials across the country to estimate the extent of forests in their counties. The information he gathered in this way was often merely impressionistic and varies substantially in accuracy from county to county and state to state. For example, the USFS currently estimates that 396.6 acres, or 89 percent, of Cheshire County, New Hampshire, is forest land. It is difficult to compare this number, based on statistical field surveys and satellite photography, with Charles Sargent's 1880 statement that "about one-half of this county is reported covered with woods" (497). Nevertheless, the reported change is large enough to justify confidence that forest cover in the county has indeed increased.

3. John W. Jordan, *Encyclopedia of Pennsylvania Biography*, vol. 12 (New York: Lewis Historical Publishing Co., 1919), 296.

4. On the role of railroads in the reshaping of the American landscape, see, for example, William Cronon, *Nature's Metropolis: Chicago and the Great West* (New York: W. W. Norton and Co., 1991); and John R. Stilgoe, *Metropolitan Corridor: Railroads and the American Scene* (New Haven, Conn.: Yale University Press, 1983).

5. Cronon, *Nature's Metropolis*.

6. With the exception of Cronon's *Changes in the Land: Indians, Colonists, and the Ecology of New England* (New York: Hill and Wang, 1983), most of the acknowl-

edged classics of U.S. environmental history, such as Cronon's *Nature's Metropolis* and the work of Richard White and Donald Worster, focus on the West. And though there has been very good recent work in northeastern environmental history, most, like *Changes in the Land*, do not focus on the twentieth century. See, for example, Theodore Steinberg, *Nature Incorporated: Industrialization and the Waters of New England* (Cambridge: Cambridge University Press, 1991). Generally, when cities have been discussed in environmental history, they have been cast in the role of villain. Although leading urban environmental historians Martin Melosi and Joel Tarr have encouraged close attention to the influences, both positive and negative, that urban people and places have on natural systems, historians' emphases have largely remained on cities' potential to pollute water and air and to spread disease. See Martin Melosi, "The Place of the City in Environmental History," *Environmental History Review* 17 (Spring 1993): 1–23. Examples of the theme of declension in environmental history are legion. To cite just a few of the most prominent: William Cronon, despite emphasizing Native American alteration of the landscape and debunking the notion of a pristine wilderness when European settlers arrived, nevertheless tells a story of decline in *Changes in the Land*. Likewise, his *Nature's Metropolis* describes a world poorer for its commodification of nature. Donald Worster, in both *Dust Bowl: The Southern Plains in the 1930s* (Oxford: Oxford University Press, 1979) and *Rivers of Empire: Water, Aridity, and the Growth of the American West* (Oxford: Oxford University Press, 1985), emphasizes a past in which agriculture was on a smaller scale and farmers worked more in harmony with the earth. Richard White, in *The Organic Machine: The Remaking of the Columbia River* (New York: Hill and Wang, 1995), and Cronon, as editor of *Uncommon Ground: Toward Reinventing Nature* (New York: W. W. Norton, 1995), have both suggested ways in which environmental historians might move away from a model of declension.

7. See, for example, Stilgoe, *Metropolitan Corridor*; Hal S. Barron, *Those Who Stayed Behind: Rural Society in Nineteenth Century New England* (Cambridge: Cambridge University Press, 1984); Michael Bell, "Did New England Really Go Downhill?" *Geographical Review* 79 (1989): 451–67; Irland, *Wildlands and Woodlots*; and Michael Williams, *Americans and Their Forests: A Historical Geography* (Cambridge: Cambridge University Press, 1989).

8. See Cronon, *Changes in the Land*, 26–27; Charles V. Cogbill, John Burk, and G. Motzkin, "The Forests of Presettlement New England, USA: Spatial and Compositional Patterns Based on Town Proprietor Surveys," *Journal of Biogeography*

29 (October and November 2002): 1295; and Stanley W. Bromley, "The Original Forest Types of Southern New England," *Ecological Monographs* 5 (January 1935): 69–70.

9. Howard W. Lull, *A Forest Atlas of the Northeast* (Upper Darby, Pa.: Northeastern Forest Experiment Station, Forest Service, U.S. Department of Agriculture, 1968), 5; and Ann Sutton and Myron Sutton, *Eastern Forests* (1985; repr., New York: Knopf, 1997), 20–27. See also, for example, Tom Wessels, *Reading the Forested Landscape: A Natural History of New England* (Woodstock, Vt.: The Countryman Press, 1997); Lloyd C. Irland, *The Northeast's Changing Forest* (Petersham, Mass.: distributed by Harvard University Press for Harvard Forest, 1999); John Elder, *Reading the Mountains of Home* (Cambridge, Mass.: Harvard University Press, 1998); and David R. Foster and John D. Aber, eds., *Forests in Time: The Environmental Consequences of 1,000 Years of Change in New England* (New Haven, Conn.: Yale University Press, 2004).

10. On urbanization, for example, see Howard P. Chudacoff and Judith E. Smith, *The Evolution of American Urban Society*, 3rd ed. (Englewood Cliffs, N.J.: Prentice Hall, 1988); Kenneth T. Jackson, *Crabgrass Frontier: The Suburbanization of the United States* (Oxford: Oxford University Press, 1985); and Joel Tarr, *The Search for the Ultimate Sink: Urban Pollution in Historical Perspective* (Akron, Ohio: University of Akron Press, 1996). On changes in rural land use, see Harold A. Meeks, *Time and Change in Vermont: A Human Geography* (Chester, Conn.: Globe Pequot Press, 1986); and Hal S. Barron, *Mixed Harvest: The Second Transformation in the Rural North, 1870–1930* (Chapel Hill: University of North Carolina Press, 1997). On forests, see Williams, *Americans and Their Forests*; and Irland, *Wildlands and Woodlots*.

11. See, for example, Char Miller, ed., *American Forests: Nature, Culture and Politics* (Lawrence: University of Kansas Press, 1997); Williams, *Americans and Their Forests*; and Harold K. Steen, ed., *The Origins of the National Forests: A Centennial Symposium* (Durham, N.C.: Forest History Society, 1992). Donald Pisani, in "Forests and Conservation, 1865–1890," in Miller, *American Forests*, 15–34, argues that new works in conservation history must "look at land and water use, and perhaps at wildlife, as well as at woodlands, and it will have to consider attitudes toward the use of natural resources throughout the nation, not just in the West" (28).

12. See, for example, Brian Donahue, *Reclaiming the Commons: Community Farms and Forests in a New England Town* (New Haven, Conn.: Yale University Press,

1999); Christopher McGrory Klyza, ed., *Wilderness Comes Home: Rewilding the Northeast* (Hanover, N.H.: University Press of New England, 2001); Christopher McGrory Klyza and Stephen C. Trombulak, *The Story of Vermont: A Natural and Cultural History* (Hanover, N.H.: University Press of New England/Middlebury College Press, 1999); and John F. O'Keefe and David Foster, "Ecological History of Massachusetts Forests," in *Stepping Forward to Look Back: A History of the Massachusetts Forest*, ed. Charles H. W. Foster (Petersham, Mass.: Harvard Forest, 1998).

13. Gregg Easterbrook, *A Moment on the Earth: The Coming Age of Environmental Optimism* (New York: Penguin Books, 1995), 11, 650; Jonathan H. Adler, "Poplar Front: The Rebirth of America's Forest," *Policy Review* 64 (Spring 1993): 87; and Bill McKibben, *Hope, Human and Wild: True Stories of Living Lightly on the Earth* (Saint Paul, Minn.: Hungry Mind Press, 1995), 16.

14. Christopher S. Wren, *Walking to Vermont: From Times Square into the Green Mountains—A Homeward Adventure* (New York: Simon & Schuster, 2004), 38, 44–45, 105, 133, 188.

15. Wren, *Walking to Vermont*, 145, 200.

ONE / WATER AND WOODS IN PENNSYLVANIA

1. Charles Fergus, *Natural Pennsylvania: Exploring the State Forest Natural Areas* (Mechanicsburg, Pa.: Stackpole Books, 2002), 63–67.

2. Ibid., 63–88; Charles Fergus, *Trees of Pennsylvania and the Northeast* (Mechanicsburg, Pa.: Stackpole Books, 2002).

3. *Annual Report of the Secretary of Internal Affairs of the Commonwealth of Pennsylvania for the Year Ending November 30, 1904* ([Harrisburg]: Wm. Stanley Ray, State Printer of Pennsylvania, 1905), B326–B327; and Douglas W. MacCleery, *American Forests: A History of Resiliency and Recovery*, revised ed. (Durham, N.C.: United States Department of Agriculture, Forest Service, with the Forest History Society, 1992; repr. 1993), 49–53.

4. "Governor Hastings' Message," *Forest Leaves* 6, no. 1 (1897): 9–11.

5. Ibid.

6. Jane Mork Gibson, *The Fairmount Waterworks* (Philadelphia: Philadelphia Museum of Art, 1988), 9; Theo B. White, *Fairmount, Philadelphia's Park: A History* (Philadelphia: Art Alliance Press, 1975); Sam Bass Warner Jr., *The Private City: Philadelphia in Its Three Periods of Growth* (Philadelphia: University

of Pennsylvania Press, 1968), 99–123; and Nelson Manfred Blake, *Water for the Cities: A History of the Urban Water Supply Problem in the United States* (Syracuse, N.Y.: Syracuse University Press, 1956), 12–13.

7. Gibson, *Fairmount Waterworks*, 9–10, 15, 29.

8. Joel Tarr, *The Search for the Ultimate Sink: Urban Pollution in Historical Perspective* (Akron, Ohio: University of Akron Press, 1996), 9; Philadelphia Water Department, *The Philadelphia Water Department: An Historical Perspective* (Philadelphia: Philadelphia Water Department, [1987]), 4; and Martin Melosi, *The Sanitary City: Urban Infrastructure in America from Colonial Times to the Present* (Baltimore: Johns Hopkins University Press, 2000), 30–35.

9. Henry Hartshorne, *Our Water Supply: What It Is, and What It Should Be: A Summary, Prepared by Request of a Committee of Citizens of Germantown, Philadelphia* (Philadelphia: Collins Printing House, 1889); Blake, *Water for the Cities*, 256–57; Russell F. Weigley, ed., *Philadelphia: A 300–Year History* (New York: W. W. Norton, 1982), 376; *Annual Report of the Bureau of Water for the Year Ending December 31, 1903* (Philadelphia: Dunlap Printing Co., 1904), xi; and James D. Ristine, *Philadelphia's Fairmount Park* (Charleston, S.C.: Arcadia, 2005), 7.

10. George Perkins Marsh, *Man and Nature, or Physical Geography as Modified by Human Action*, ed. David Lowenthal (Cambridge, Mass.: Harvard University Press, Belknap Press, 1965; first published 1864); and Hartshorne, *Our Water Supply*.

11. Lisa W. Foderaro, "Buying Woodland and Meadow to Save the City's Water," *New York Times*, 20 December 2003; "EPA Spares NYC Cost of Building Water Filtration Plant: Agency Rules City Can Go 10 Years without Constructing a Facility," *Albany Times Union*, 15 April 2007; Diane Dumanoski, "MWRA Postpones Wachusett Filtration Plant," *Boston Globe*, 10 June 1993; and Michael Levenson, "Water Has MWRA Bubbling with Joy: New Process Said to Improve Taste," *Boston Globe*, 20 August 2005.

12. Gibson, *Fairmount Waterworks*, 38.

13. Sue Anne Prince, ed., "Stuffing Birds, Pressing Plants, Shaping Knowledge: Natural History in North America," special issue, *Transactions of the American Philosophical Society* 93, pt. 4 (2003): 1–8.

14. Robert McCracken Peck, "Alcohol and Arsenic, Pepper and Pitch: Brief Histories of Preservation Techniques," in Prince, "Stuffing Birds," 47–48; Joyce Elizabeth Chaplin, "Nature and Nation: Natural History in Context," in Prince, "Stuffing Birds," 65; and Murray Murphy, *City Chronicles: Science and Technology in Philadelphia* (Philadelphia: Philadelphia '76 Inc., 1976), 4.

15. Murphy, *City Chronicles*, 6, 11, 21; M. Albert Linton, *The Academy of Natural Sciences of Philadelphia: 150 Years of Distinguished Service* (New York: Newcomen Society in North America, 1962); and Gretchen Worden, *Mutter Museum of the College of Physicians of Philadelphia* (New York: Blast Books, 2002), 10.

16. See, for example, Roderick Nash, *Wilderness and the American Mind* (New Haven, Conn.: Yale University Press, 1967), 67–107; Thomas R. Cox, Robert S. Maxwell, Phillip Drennon Thomas, and Joseph P. Malone, *This Well-Wooded Land: Americans and Their Forests from Colonial Times to the Present* (Lincoln: University of Nebraska Press, 1985), 134–35; Michael Williams, *Americans and Their Forests: A Historical Geography* (Cambridge: Cambridge University Press, 1989), 16–18; Donald Worster, *Nature's Economy: A History of Ecological Ideas*, 2nd ed. (Cambridge: Cambridge University Press, 1994; first published 1977); and Marsh, *Man and Nature*.

17. Marsh, *Man and Nature*; Cox et al., *This Well-Wooded Land*, 144; and Stephen C. Trombulak, ed., *So Great a Vision: The Conservation Writings of George Perkins Marsh* (Hanover, N.H.: University Press of New England, 2001), ix–xviii.

18. Cox et al., *This Well-Wooded Land*, 145.

19. See Richard W. Judd, *Common Lands, Common People: The Origins of Conservation in Northern New England* (Cambridge, Mass.: Harvard University Press, 1997), 90–99; John F. Reiger, *American Sportsmen and the Origins of Conservation* (Norman: University of Oklahoma Press, 1986); Harold K. Steen, "The Origins and Significance of the National Forest System," in *The Origins of the National Forests: A Centennial Symposium*, ed. Harold K. Steen (Durham, N.C.: Forest History Society, 1992), 4–7; and Samuel P. Hays, *Conservation and the Gospel of Efficiency* (Cambridge, Mass: Harvard University Press, 1959; repr., Pittsburgh: University of Pittsburgh Press, 1999), 1–48. On page 27, Hays explains that the original members of the American Forestry Association were primarily "botanists, landscape gardeners, and estate owners, . . . [who] emphasized arboriculture, an aesthetic appreciation of forests, and the study of individual trees. It displayed more concern for saving trees from destruction than for efficient timber management." See also Williams, *Americans and Their Forests*, 404–5.

20. Simon Baatz, "Philadelphia Patronage: The Institutional Structure of Natural History in the New Republic, 1800–1833," *Journal of the Early Republic* 8, no. 2 (Summer 1988): 111–38.

21. Quoted in Baatz, "Philadelphia Patronage," 121.

22. Baatz, "Philadelphia Patronage," 121.

23. William G. Robbins, *American Forestry: A History of National, State and Private Cooperation* (Lincoln: University of Nebraska Press, 1985), 3–7; and Cox et al., *This Well-Wooded Land*, 147–48.

24. See, for example, Char Miller, *Gifford Pinchot and the Making of Modern Environmentalism* (Washington, D.C.: Island Press, 2001).

25. See, for example, Hays, *Conservation and the Gospel of Efficiency*, 122–23.

26. Williams, *Americans and Their Forests*, 380–81; Cox et al., *This Well-Wooded Land*, 144–45.

27. Philip G. Terrie, "The Adirondack Forest Preserve: The Irony of Forever Wild," *New York History* (July 1981): 266; J. T. Rothrock, *Areas of Desolation in Pennsylvania* (Philadelphia: Herbert Welsh, 1915), 9; Howard W. Lull, "Forest Influences: Growth of a Concept," *Journal of Forestry* 47 (September 1949): 700–705; and "To Protect Forests," *Baltimore News*, 21 January 1903, clipping, box 4, folder 34, Mira Dock Collection, Pennsylvania State Archives, Harrisburg (hereafter cited as MDC). Although scientists no longer believe that trees "attract" rain, there is new evidence that trees' absorption and transpiration of water can significantly affect the humidity of an area. Water that would otherwise drain immediately into a river in the absence of tree cover will instead be absorbed by trees and then released back into the atmosphere. A single birch tree, for example, may absorb and release as much as three hundred liters of water a day. See Peter Thomas, *Trees: Their Natural History* (Cambridge: Cambridge University Press, 2000), 13–18.

28. Account book of Joseph T. Rothrock, Commissioner of Forestry, 1897–1904, record group 6, Department of Forestry and Waters, Pennsylvania State Archives, Harrisburg.

29. *Annual Report of the Bureau of Water for the Year Ending December 31, 1895* (Philadelphia: Dunlap Printing Co., 1896), 100; Henry P. M. Birkinbine, "The Future Water Supply of Philadelphia," *Journal of the Franklin Institute* (1878): 11, in the collection of the Historical Society of Pennsylvania; and Dr. C. M. Cresson to S. S. Hollingsworth, 27 December 1886, *The Water Supply of Philadelphia: Communications from Charles M. Cresson, M.D. and Albert R. Leeds, Ph.D.* (Philadelphia: Allen, Lane & Scott, Printers, 1887), 6, 7, in the collection of the Historical Society of Pennsylvania.

30. James O. Handy to Herbert Welsh, 25 April 1893, box 88 (Pure Water and Sanitation), folder H–J (1893), HWC (see intro., n. 1); "Circular of the Union Committee to Secure an Adequate Water Supply for Philadelphia and to Pro-

mote Municipal Sanitation," box 88, folder Pure Water and Sanitation 1893 T–Z (1893), HWC; extract of a letter from Dr. William H. Ford, President of the City Board of Health, 5 May 1893, box 88, folder F–G (1893), HWC; and Tarr, *The Search for the Ultimate Sink,* 95.

31. *Report of the Water Supply Commission, 1905–1906* (Harrisburg: Harrisburg Publishing Co., State Printer, 1907), 3, 4, 10, 11.

32. *Pennsylvania Laws,* 1893, p. 115, no. 68.

33. *Pennsylvania Laws,* 1897, p. 11, no. 10.

34. Susan Dudley and David R. Goddard, "Joseph T. Rothrock and Forest Conservation," *Proceedings of the American Philosophical Society* 117, no. 1 (February 16, 1973): 37–50; and J. T. Rothrock, "On the Growth of the Forestry Idea in Pennsylvania," *Proceedings of the American Philosophical Society* 32, no. 143, Commemoration of the One Hundred and Fiftieth Anniversary of the Foundation of the American Philosophical Society (January 1894): 332–42.

35. Joseph T. Rothrock, *Preliminary Report of the Commissioner of Forestry for 1896. Also Miscellaneous Papers on Forestry Contained in Annual Report, Department of Agriculture, for 1896* ([Harrisburg]: Harrisburg Publishing Co., State Printer, 1897), 4.

36. *Philadelphia Board of Trade, Annual Report 1894* (Philadelphia: Burk & McFetridge, Printers, 1894), 32–33.

37. Rothrock, *Preliminary Report* (1897), 7.

38. Ibid., 8.

39. Lester A. DeCoster, *The Legacy of Penn's Woods: A History of the Pennsylvania Bureau of Forestry* ([Harrisburg]: Commonwealth of Pennsylvania, Pennsylvania Historical and Museum Commission, 1995), x. See John G. Stephenson III, "Land Office Business in Pennsylvania," *Villanova Law Review* 4, no. 2 (Winter 1958–59): 175–97; and *Annual Report of the Secretary of Internal Affairs of the Commonwealth of Pennsylvania for the Year Ending November 30, 1904,* A18–A23.

40. Rothrock's Account Book.

41. Ibid. Forest acquisition information in Pennsylvania Bureau of Forestry Forest Resource Plans, 1985–99 (20 volumes, one for each forest, are located in the Pennsylvania Department of Natural Resources Library); and *The Atlas of Pennsylvania* (Philadelphia: Temple University Press, 1989), 93.

42. *Atlas of Pennsylvania,* 95. By 1920 Pennsylvania's rank among timber harvesting states had slid to nineteen; in 1939 it ranked thirty-fourth.

43. Rothrock's Account Book; and "Tabular State Forest Acquisition List," files

of Daniel Devlin, chief of resource planning, Bureau of Forestry, Pennsylvania Department of Conservation and Natural Resources. Pennsylvania's tax laws were finally changed in 1913 to encourage the maintenance of forests on privately held land. See Louis S. Murphy, P. A. Herbert, and Wade E. DeVries, *Digest of Forest Tax Laws in the United States in Effect January 1, 1932*, Progress Report of the Forest Taxation Inquiry, no. 16 ([Washington, D.C.]: United States Department of Agriculture, Forest Service, 1932), 46–48.

44. Pennsylvania Land Office Records, file 3, nos. 14, 15, 45 (deeds from R. W. A. Jameson, Clinton County treasurer, to Pennsylvania Forestry Commission); *Pennsylvania Laws*, 1905, p. 67, no. 50; and "Tabular State Forest Acquisition List."

45. DeCoster, *Legacy of Penn's Woods*, 11–15.

46. Ernest Morrison, *J. Horace McFarland: A Thorn for Beauty* (Harrisburg: Pennsylvania Historical and Museum Commission, 1995), 71; "Miss Dock Appointed," *Harrisburg Telegraph*, 25 July 1901, box 4, folder 34, MDC; and Susan Rimby, "'Better Housekeeping Out of Doors': Mira Lloyd Dock, the State Federation of Pennsylvania Women, and Progressive Era Conservation," *Journal of Women's History* 17, no. 3 (2005): 9–34.

47. "To Protect Forests," *Baltimore News*, 21 January 1903, clipping, box 4, folder 34, MDC.

48. "An Evening of Entertainment: Miss Dock Addressed the Clio Club," *Williamsport, Pa., Gazette*, 28 April 1899, clipping, box 4, folder 34, MDC.

49. "Miss Dock Appointed"; Pennsylvania Laws 1893, p. 115, no. 68; and "To Protect Forests."

50. Morrison, *Thorn for Beauty*, 71.

51. "To Protect Forests"; "Women and Their Interests: Chief Events of the Week in the Leading Clubs, Home Thoughts, Household Suggestions, and a Review of the Fashions: Women's Club News," *New York Evening Post*, 10 February 1906, clipping; and "Pleads for Forests: Miss Lloyd Dock Lectures before Arundell Club," *Baltimore Sun*, 22 January 1903, all in box 4, folder 34, MDC.

52. Morrison, *Thorn for Beauty*, 72–73.

53. Quoted in Morrison, *Thorn for Beauty*, 73.

54. Morrison, *Thorn for Beauty*, 73.

55. Ibid., 83–84.

56. J. Horace McFarland to Mira L. Dock, 26 September 1905, MG–85, container 1 (Private Papers), Pennsylvania Historical and Museum Commission, Harrisburg.

57. Morrison, *Thorn for Beauty*, 78–80, 83.

58. DeCoster, *Legacy of Penn's Woods*, 42–43. It is difficult to say how many acres were replanted, since the proper spacing between seedlings was a point of debate at the turn of the century. Current standards for softwood planting for timber production call for between 600 and 1,000 trees per acre; some early plantings had as few as 350 trees per acre, others as many as 2,300.

59. "Tabular State Forest Acquisition List"; and Carol L. Alerich, *Forest Statistics for Pennsylvania, 1978 and 1989* (Radnor, Pa.: United States Department of Agriculture, Forest Service, Northeastern Forest Experiment Station, January 1993), table 146.

60. Mira Dock to Thomas Will, 3 March 1908, box 5, folder 51, MDC.

61. R. Y. Stuart, secretary, Pennsylvania Department of Forests and Waters, "The State Forests of Pennsylvania," *Pennsylvania Department of Forests and Waters, Bulletin 37* (March 1925); *The Delaware State Forest Public Use Map* (Harrisburg: Commonwealth of Pennsylvania Department of Conservation and Natural Resources, 1998); and watershed management information in Pennsylvania Bureau of Forestry Forest Resource Plans, 1985–99.

62. Melosi, *Sanitary City*, 30–31; see also Donald Worster, *Nature's Economy*.

63. Alerich, *Forest Statistics for Pennsylvania*, table 146; *Annual Report of the Secretary of Internal Affairs of the Commonwealth of Pennsylvania for the Year Ending November 30, 1904*, B326–B327; Douglas W. MacCleery, *American Forests*, 49–53; and Paul Nussbaum, "A Lush Renewal for Pa. Forests," *Philadelphia Inquirer*, 16 August 1998.

64. See Terrie, "Adirondack Forest Preserve," 261–88; Sarah S. Elkind, *Bay Cities and Water Politics: The Battle for Resources in Boston and Oakland* (Lawrence: University Press of Kansas, 1998); and Nelson Manfred Blake, *Water for the Cities: A History of the Urban Water Supply Problem in the United States* (New York: Syracuse University Press, 1956). See also William A. Healy, "History of Water Supplies in New Hampshire, 1882–1957," 122–26; Warren J. Scott, "Seventy-Five Years of Water-Works Progress in Connecticut," 127–33; Walter J. Shea, "Seventy-Five Years of Water-Works Progress in Rhode Island," 134–37; and Edward L. Tracy, "Seventy-Five Years of Water-Works Progress in Vermont," 143–48, all in *Journal of the New England Water Works Association* (June 1958).

65. Terrie, "Adirondack Forest Preserve"; J. B. Harrison to Herbert Welsh, 14 March 1890, box 74 (Forestry) folder B–L (1890), HWC; J. B. Harrison to Herbert Welsh, 31 December 1892, box 74 (Forestry) folder B–L (1892), HWC; Sunapee Circular Subscription List, box 75 (Forestry) folder A–W (1918), HWC;

"Sketch of the Forestry Movement in Philadelphia," *Forest Leaves* (July 1886): 1; "Private Forestry Preservation," *Forest Leaves* (January 1889): 6; Pennsylvania Forestry Association Membership List, *Forest Leaves* (May 1892): 130–33; and William H. Rivers, "Massachusetts State Forestry Programs," in *Stepping Back to Look Forward: A History of the Massachusetts Forest*, ed. Charles H. W. Foster (Cambridge, Mass.: Harvard University Press, 1998), 176.

TWO / NEW HAMPSHIRE WATERSHEDS, VIEWSHEDS, AND TIMBER

1. Allen Hollis to Herbert Welsh, 27 September 1909, box 74 (Forestry), folder B–W (1909), HWC (see intro., n. 1); Philip Ayres, *Manual of Mount Sunapee* (New York: Knickerbocker Press, 1915), 1, 2; Philip Ayres, "The Forest on Suna-pee Mountain," folder B–W 1909, box 74 (Forestry), HWC; Philip Ayres to Allen Hollis, 13 November 1909, folder B–W (1909), box 74 (Forestry), HWC; B. C. White to Herbert Welsh, 21 December 1909, folder B–W (1909), box 74 (Forestry), HWC; "New York Members of Society for Protection of New Hampshire Forests," folder 1894 (apparently misfiled), box 74 (Forestry), HWC; memo and list of contributions, folder B–W (1909), box 74 (Forestry), HWC; and George Dewey to M. K. Sniffen, 12 October 1910, folder B–D (1910) box 74 (Forestry), HWC.

2. Klyza, "The Northern Forest," 39 (see intro., n. 2); and W. R. Brown, Chairman, State Forestry Commission, State of New Hampshire, Forestry Department, "Forest Resources of New Hampshire," *Report of the Forestry Commission,* January 1923, box 8, folder 37, Society for the Protection of New Hampshire Forests Collection, Milne Special Collections and Archives, University of New Hampshire Library, Durham (hereafter cited as SPNHF). See also, for example, McK-ibben, *Hope, Human and Wild* (see intro., n. 13); and Dona Brown, *Inventing New England: Regional Tourism in the Nineteenth Century* (Washington, D.C.: Smithsonian Institution Press, 1995).

3. Sunapee Historical Society, *Sunapee New Hampshire Bicentennial, 1768–1968: Historical Pictures and Stories* (Sunapee, N.H.: Common Sense Marketing, n.d., reproduced from 1968 edition), 16; "Lake Sunapee Area Hotels and Inns," cal-endar (Sunapee, N.H.: SooNipi, 1999); and "Sunapee Mountain House," photo, Collection of J. Hutchinson, Common Sense Marketing, Sunapee, N.H.

4. Harold Fisher Wilson, *The Hill Country of Northern New England: Its Social and Economic History, 1790–1930* (New York: Columbia University Press, 1936), 16–18;

and Nancy Coffey Heffernan and Ann Page Stecker, *New Hampshire: Crosscurrents in Its Development* (Grantham, N.H.: Thompson and Rutter, 1986), 87–93.

5. Heffernan and Stecker, *New Hampshire*, 94.

6. Heffernan and Stecker, *New Hampshire*, 93; and Wilson, *Hill Country*, 26.

7. Wilson, *Hill Country*, 100.

8. Theodore Steinberg, *Nature Incorporated: Industrialization and the Waters of New England* (Amherst: University of Massachusetts Press, 1991), 57, 59, 79.

9. Philip Ayres, "The Commercial Importance of the White Mountain Forests," *USDA Forest Service Circular* 168, 4 November (Washington, D.C.: Government Printing Office, 1909), 3; and Heffernan and Stecker, *New Hampshire*, 142.

10. Workers of the Federal Writers' Project of the Works Progress Administration for the State of New Hampshire, *New Hampshire: A Guide to the Granite State* (Boston: Houghton Mifflin, 1938), 23; Christine Lynn Goodale, "The Long-Term Effects of Disturbance on Nitrogen Cycling and Loss in the White Mountains, New Hampshire" (PhD diss., University of New Hampshire, 1999), 6; Wilson, *Hill Country*, 46–47; and Richard Judd, *Common Lands, Common People: The Origins of Conservation in Northern New England* (Cambridge, Mass.: Harvard University Press, 1997), 199.

11. Gerald Ogden, "Forestry for a Nation: The Making of a National Forest Policy under the Weeks and Clarke-McNary Acts, 1900–1924" (PhD. diss., University of New Mexico, 1980), 89; and Harold K. Steen, "The Beginning of the National Forest System," in *American Forests: Nature, Culture, and Politics*, ed. Char Miller (Lawrence: University Press of Kansas, 1997), 53.

12. Sunapee Historical Society, *Sunapee New Hampshire Bicentennial*, 16.

13. Donald E. MacAskill, "Mt. Sunapee State Park: A Comprehensive History" (manuscript, Abbott Library, Sunapee, N. H., 18 May 1981), 19–25; and State Board of Agriculture, *Official List of Summer Hotels and Boarding Houses in New Hampshire, 1897* (Concord, N.H.: Edward N. Pearson, Public Printer, 1897), 16.

14. New Hampshire Board of Agriculture, *Annual Report of the Board of Agriculture from May 1, 1889 to December 1, 1890*, by N. J. Bachelder, Secretary (Manchester, N.H.: John B. Clarke, Public Printer, 1890), 472–73.

15. New Hampshire Board of Agriculture, *Annual Report 1889 to 1890*, 473; New Hampshire Board of Agriculture, *New Hampshire Farms for Summer Homes* (Concord, N.H.: Ira C. Evans, Public Printer, 1894), 3; and New Hampshire Board of Agriculture, *New Hampshire Farms for Summer Homes*, 8th ed. (Concord, N.H.: Rumford Press, 1910), 7.

16. New Hampshire Board of Agriculture, *Annual Report 1889 to 1890*, 473, 477, 478. Quotation is from page 478.

17. New Hampshire Board of Agriculture, *Annual Report 1889 to 1890*, 6, 473 (quotation is from page 6); New Hampshire State Board of Labor, *The Summer Season in New Hampshire: Special Report of the Summer Boarding Business and Resorts in New Hampshire, 1899* (Manchester, N.H.: Arthur E. Clarke, Public Printer, 1900), viii–x; and New Hampshire State Board of Labor, *Second Special Report of the Summer Boarding Business and Resorts in New Hampshire, 1905* (Concord, N.H.: State Bureau of Labor, 1906), ix.

18. Howard Lull, *A Forest Atlas of the Northeast* (Upper Darby, Pa.: Northeastern Forest Experiment Station, United States Department of Agriculture, Forest Service, 1968), 5.

19. State of New Hampshire Forestry Commission, *Wood-Using Industries of New Hampshire* (Concord, N.H.: Ira C. Evans Co., Printers, 1912), 39; and George Draper to Mrs. John Hay, 7 December 1910, box 74 (Forestry), folder B–D (1910), HWC.

20. Constitution of New Hampshire, part 2, article 5; State of New Hampshire, *Biennial Report of the Forestry Commission for the Two Fiscal Years Ending August 31, 1920* (Manchester, N.H.: John B. Clarke, 1920), 85–87. According to Wilson Compton, in "Tendencies in the Reform of Forest Taxation," *Journal of Political Economy* 23 (1915): 971–79, early efforts to amend the constitution were defeated "mainly through the efforts of large wood-using corporations interested in the purchase of timber at low prices from heavily taxed owners."

21. Fred Rogers Fairchild, *Forest Taxation in the United States*, Miscellaneous Publication No. 218, (Washington, D.C.: United States Department of Agriculture, October 1935), 355.

22. J. B. Harrison to Herbert Welsh, 14 March 1890, box 74 (Forestry), folder B–L (1890), HWC.

23. J. B. Harrison to Herbert Welsh, 19 April 1893, folder B–R (1893); and J. B. Harrison to Herbert Welsh, 8 December 1892, folder B–L (1892), both in box 74 (Forestry), HWC.

24. J. B. Harrison to Herbert Welsh, 10 December 1892; and J. B. Harrison to Herbert Welsh, 23 December 1892, both in box 74 (Forestry), folder B–L (1892), HWC.

25. J. B. Harrison to Herbert Welsh, 10 December 1892.

26. J. B. Harrison to Herbert Welsh, 8 December 1892, box 74 (Forestry), folder B–L (1892), HWC.

27. J. B. Harrison to Herbert Welsh, 23 December 1892.

28. J. B. Harrison to Herbert Welsh, 8 December 1892.

29. J. B. Harrison to Herbert Welsh, 8 December 1892; and J. B. Harrison to Herbert Welsh, 10 December 1892.

30. J. B. Harrison to Herbert Welsh, 8 December 1892.

31. J. B. Harrison to Herbert Welsh, 23 December 1892; J. B. Harrison to Herbert Welsh, 31 December 1892, folder B–L (1892); and J. B. Harrison to Herbert Welsh, 4 February 1893, folder B–R (1893), all in box 74 (Forestry), HWC.

32. Edward Charles Murphy et al., "Destructive Floods in the United States in 1905 with a Discussion of Flood Discharge and Frequency and an Index to Flood Literature," *United States Geological Survey Water Supply Paper #162* (Washington, D.C.: GPO, 1906), 58; William Shands, "The Lands Nobody Wanted: The Legacy of the Eastern National Forests," in *The Origins of the National Forests: A Centennial Symposium*, ed. Harold K. Steen (Durham, N.C.: Forest History Society, 1992), 27; "Raging Waters: Flood of Unprecedented Volume Sweeps All Before It," *Concord Evening Monitor*, 3 March 1896 (first quotation); and "Waters Fast Receding," *Manchester Union*, 4 March 1896 (second quotation).

33. "Waters Fast Receding"; and "Havoc of Raging Floods Is Widespread Throughout New England States," *Boston Herald*, 4 March 1896.

34. "Havoc of Raging Floods"; and "First Spring Freshet: Many New England Towns Inundated: Damage Already Reaches Million. Seven Lives Lost in Different States. Thousands of Operatives Idle at Lowell and Haverhill," *Boston Evening Transcript*, 2 March 1896.

35. David E. Conrad, *The Land We Cared For: A History of the Forest Service's Eastern Region* (Milwaukee, Wis.: United States Department of Agriculture, Forest Service, Region 9, 1997), 29–30.

36. "The Lesson of It," *Manchester Union*, 6 March 1896.

37. Ibid.

38. Martha Carlson and Richard Ober, "The Weeks Act," *Forest Notes* (Summer 1998): 4.

39. Meyer Berger, *The Story of the New York Times, 1851–1951* (New York: Simon and Schuster, 1951), 112; and "The Critical Moment in the White Mountains," *New York Times*, 21 November 1892 (quotation from the *New York Times*).

40. "Devastating the White Mountains," *New York Times*, 13 November 1892.

41. Judd, *Common Lands, Common People*, 104; and Ogden, "Forestry for a Nation," 112.

42. See, for example, Philip W. Ayres, *Forest Problems in New Hampshire*, reprinted from *Forestry Quarterly* (July 1903) for the Society for the Protection of New Hampshire Forests, box 2, folder 34; "In the Statement on the Physical Relation Between Forests and Stream Flow in the Appalachian Region," statement before the Committee on Agriculture of the House of Representatives, Thursday, 30 January 1908, box 31, folder 26; "Organizations That Supported the Weeks Act," box 31, folder 26; and Resolution, American Paper and Pulp Association, box 31, folder 27, all in SPNHF.

43. Ayres, *Forest Problems in New Hampshire*, 6.

44. Philip Ayres, "National Forests in the Eastern Mountains" [1923?], p. 2, box 31, folder 26, SPNHF.

45. Ayres, *Forest Problems in New Hampshire*, 6–7.

46. See, for example, Ogden, "Forestry for a Nation," 198; and Michael Williams, *Americans and Their Forests: A Historical Geography* (Cambridge: Cambridge University Press, 1989), 406–7.

47. Ayres, *Forest Problems in New Hampshire*, 6.

48. Ayres, "National Forests in the Eastern Mountains," 2.

49. Judd, *Common Lands, Common People*, 104; Ayres, "National Forests in the Eastern Mountains"; and Ogden, "Forestry for a Nation," 115, 148.

50. Allen Hollis to Herbert Welsh, 27 September 1909, box 74 (Forestry), folder B–W 1909, HWC; and MacAskill, "Mt. Sunapee State Park," 24.

51. Philip Ayres to Herbert Welsh, 18 October 1909, folder B–W (1909); Philip Ayres to Herbert Welsh, 3 November 1909, folder B–W (1909); Philip Ayres to Allen Hollis, 13 November 1909, folder B–W (1909); Geo. W. Dewey to Philip Ayres, 3 January 1910, folder Ayres, P. (Jan.–Apr. 1910); and "Memorandum of a Meeting Held at the Faculty Club, Columbia University, Saturday, January 15, 1910, Relative to Sunapee Mountain," folder Ayres, P. (Jan.–Apr. 1910), all in box 74 (Forestry), HWC.

52. "We Present," *Journal of Forestry* 43, no. 11 (November 1945): 843.

53. Philip Ayres to Herbert Welsh, 8 January 1910; Philip Ayres to George Dewey, 10 January 1910; and "Memorandum of a Meeting Held at the Faculty Club, Columbia University, Saturday, January 15, 1910, Relative to Sunapee Mountain", all in box 74 (Forestry), folder Ayres, P. (Jan.–Apr. 1910), HWC.

54. Philip W. Ayres to Herbert Welsh, 20 May 1912, box 74 (Forestry), folder Ayres, P. (1907) (apparently misfiled); Philip Ayres to Herbert Welsh, 15 June 1912, box 75 (Forestry), folder Ayres, P. (1912); Philip Ayres to Herbert Welsh, 15 July 1911,

box 74 (Forestry), folder Ayres, P. (May–Oct. 1910) (apparently misfiled); and Herbert Welsh to Frank R. Shipman, 25 August 1911, box 75 (Forestry), folder S–W (1911), all in HWC.

55. Philip Ayres to Allen Hollis, 14 April 1910, folder Ayres, P. (Jan.–Apr. 1910); Philip Ayres to A. D. Felch, 20 April 1910, folder Ayres, P. (Jan.–Apr. 1910); Copy of extract from deed, Emerson Paper Company to Draper Company, 28 December 1908, folder Ayres, P. (Nov.–Dec. 1910); and Ayres, "Forest on Sunapee Mountain," folder B–W (1909), all in box 74 (Forestry), HWC.

56. Ayres, "National Forests in the Eastern Mountains" (quotation from page 3); and Shands, "Lands Nobody Wanted," 34, 35. On the roles of watershed protection and broad coalitions in the creation of the White Mountain National Forest, see Judd, *Common Lands, Common People*, 99–111.

57. Workers of the Federal Writers' Project of the Works Progress Administration, *New Hampshire*, 23, 512; and Shands, "Lands Nobody Wanted," 31. See also Kimberly A. Jarvis, *Franconia Notch and the Women Who Saved It* (Durham: University of New Hampshire Press, 2007).

58. Philip W. Ayres, *Forest Preservation in the Eastern Mountains* (Boston: Society for the Protection of New Hampshire Forests, [1920]), reprinted from *American Review of Reviews* (April 1920), box 2, folder 34, SPNHF.

THREE / PACKAGING THE FORESTED FARM IN VERMONT

1. See Blake Harrison, *The View from Vermont: Tourism and the Making of an American Rural Landscape* (Burlington: University of Vermont Press, 2006).

2. Vermont State Board of Agriculture, *Beautiful Vermont: Unsurpassed as a Residence or Playground . . .* (Woodstock, Vt.: State Board of Agriculture, 1907), cover, 7. Both quotations are from page 7.

3. Dona Brown, in *Inventing New England: Regional Tourism in the Nineteenth Century* (Washington, D.C.: Smithsonian Institution Press, 1995), writes, "Spear's enterprise was filled with irony. In order to reserve the Vermont farm as a haven against speculation and greed, Spear pressed farmers to rationalize production, delve more deeply into speculative involvements in the market, and finally to plunge into what was probably the most modernizing and disruptive business available to them: the tourist industry. To safeguard the home and its values, Spear encouraged farmers to bring the forces of urbanism into those very homes" (148–49).

4. Andrea Rebek, "The Selling of Vermont: From Agriculture to Tourism, 1860–1910," *Vermont History* 44 (1976): 27.

5. Vermont Bureau of Publicity, *Vermont Farms: Some Facts and Figures Concerning the Agricultural Resources and Opportunities of the Green Mountain State* (St. Johnsbury, Vt.: Caledonia, [1916]), 110.

6. Echo Lake Hotel, *Echo Lake Hotel, Tyson, Vermont*, advertising booklet (1908), 10, 16.

7. Bertha Oppenheim, *Winged Seeds* (New York: Macmillan, 1923), 1, 3, 4; and Arthur Wallace Peach, *Contemporary Vermont Writers* (Northfield, Vt.: Norwich University Publications, June 1927), 45. *Winged Seeds* is one of many early twentieth-century memoirs of city people seeking and cultivating Vermont country retreats. Elswyth Thane, in her memoir *The Reluctant Farmer* (New York: Duell, Sloan and Pearce, 1950), refers to the genre dismissively as "I-bought-a-barn" books. (Thane claims to distinguish herself from the throngs through a lack of romanticism. "We didn't search long, we didn't give a hoot about a barn, and we didn't meet any quaint characters while we were looking" [14].)

8. Oppenheim, *Winged Seeds*, 3–5, 7, 8, 96.

9. Ibid., 4, 8, 26, 28, 90.

10. N. H. Egleston, "Facts and Figures in Respect to the Forests of the Country and Their Consumption," *Proceedings of the American Forestry Congress, Boston, September 1885* (Washington, D.C.: Judd and Detwiller, Printers, 1886). The table in this publication lists Vermont as being 32.5 percent forested, as a percentage of all potentially forested land—that is, the total acreage considered did not include urban areas or lakes.

11. R. S. Kellogg, *The Timber Supply of the United States*, Forest Service Circular 97 (Washington, D.C.: United States Department of Agriculture, 1907), 14; *Report on the Productions of Agriculture as Returned at the Tenth Census (June 1, 1880), Embracing General Statistics* (Washington, D.C.: Government Printing Office, 1883), 12; and *Fourteenth Census of the United States taken in the Year 1920, Volume V: Agriculture. General Report and Analytical Tables* (Washington, D.C.: Government Printing Office, 1992), 17. The definition of "other unimproved land" comes from page 17 of the 1920 census, but conveys the same concept as far wordier explanations in the 1883 volume, pages 8–14.

12. *Fourteenth Census of the United States taken in the Year 1920, Volume V: Agriculture. General Report and Analytical Tables*, 35, 37; Christopher McGrory Klyza, "The Northern Forest: Problems, Politics and Alternatives," in *The Future of the*

Northern Forest, ed. Christopher McGrory Klyza and Stephen C. Trombulak (Hanover, N.H.: University Press of New England, 1994), 39; Lloyd C. Irland, *Wildlands and Woodlots: The Story of New England's Forests* (Hanover, N.H.: University Press of New England, 1982), 2; and United States Department of Agriculture, Forest Service, National (FIA) Forest Inventory and Analysis Databases, "Forest Inventory Data Online (FIDO)," http://apps.fs.fed.us/fido (data accessed spring 2001).

13. William J. Wilgus, *The Role of Transportation in the Development of Vermont* (Montpelier: Vermont Historical Society, 1945), 13. See also Harold Meeks, *Time and Change in Vermont* (Chester, Conn.: Globe Pequot Press, 1986), 106–39.

14. Wilgus, *Role of Transportation*, 42.

15. Ibid., 14, 30, 63.

16. Ibid., 54, 63, 66, 97–99. The major railroads in Vermont in the late nineteenth and early twentieth century were the Central Vermont Railway (opened in 1848), the Rutland Railroad (opened in 1849), the Boston and Maine Railroad (opened in 1848), the Maine Central–St. Johnsbury and Lake Champlain Railroad (opened in 1872), the Montpelier and Wells Railroad (opened in 1873), and the Delaware and Hudson Railroad (opened in 1850). Numerous smaller railroads served rural areas. See Vermont Historical Society, *Map of Railroads in Vermont*, 1944.

17. Leland Spencer and Charles J. Blanford, *An Economic History of Milk Marketing and Pricing: A Classified Bibliography with Reviews of Listed Publications, 1840–1970* (Columbus, Ohio: Grid, 1973), 690.

18. Ibid., 700.

19. Ibid., 690.

20. Leland Spencer, *The Surplus Problem in the Northeastern Milksheds*, Bulletin No. 24 ([Washington, D.C.?]: New York State College of Agriculture, in cooperation with Cooperative Division, Farm Credit Administration, April 1938), 5. The northeastern states included in this average are Maine, New Hampshire, Vermont, Massachusetts, Connecticut, Rhode Island, New York, New Jersey, Pennsylvania, Maryland, and Delaware.

21. Spencer, *Surplus Problem*, 9, 12.

22. John M. Cassels, *A Study of Fluid Milk Prices* (Cambridge, Mass.: Harvard University Press, 1937), 150.

23. Ibid., 143, 151–53.

24. See Brown, *Inventing New England*, 148–54.

25. Christopher McGrory Klyza and Stephen C. Trombulak, *The Story of Vermont: A*

Natural and Cultural History (Hanover, N.H.: University Press of New England, 1999), 109.

26. See, for example, Passenger Department of the Central Vermont Railroad, *Summer Homes Among the Green Hills of Vermont and Along the Shores of Lake Champlain* (St. Albans, Vt.: Messenger and Advertiser Job Print, 1891); Boston and Maine Railroad, *Memphremagog Region*, pamphlet located at the New York Public Library (General Passenger Division, Boston and Maine Railroad, [late nineteenth-century]); Vermont Board of Agriculture, *A List of Desirable Farms and Summer Homes in Vermont* (Montpelier, Vt.: Watchman, 1895); and Vermont State Board of Agriculture, *Beautiful Vermont*.

27. Oppenheim, *Winged Seeds*, 7.

28. Central Vermont Railroad, *Summer Homes* (1891).

29. Passenger Department of the Central Vermont Railroad, *Summer Homes Among the Green Hills of Vermont, Islands and Shores of Lake Champlain, Adirondacks and Canada, reached by the Popular Green Mountain Route* (Troy, N.Y.: Troy Times Art Press, 1902), 6–7.

30. Ibid., 6.

31. Tennie Gaskill Toussaint, "The Doles of Dole Hill," *Vermont History* 22 (1954): 291.

32. Wallace Nutting, *Vermont Beautiful* (Framingham, Vt.: Old America, 1922), 37.

33. Ibid., 37, 102.

34. Ibid., 114, 117.

35. Klyza and Trombulak, *Story of Vermont*, 55, 92, 93; Charles S. Sargent, *Report on the Forests of North America (exclusive of Mexico), Tenth Census of the United States, 1880* (Washington, D.C.: Government Printing Office, 1884), 498–99; and Ralph Nading Hill, *Yankee Kingdom: Vermont and New Hampshire* (New York: Harper and Brothers, 1960), 172.

36. Klyza and Trombulak, *Story of Vermont*, 6, 95–96; Perry H. Merrill, *History of Forestry in Vermont, 1909–1959* (Montpelier, Vt.: State Board of Forests and Parks, 1959), 11, 29; and Austin F. Hawes, State Forester for Connecticut, "Forestry, the Salvation of a Worn-out Connecticut Town," *New England Magazine* 39 (September 1908): 19–25. By 1948, over thirty million trees from the nursery had been planted in Vermont.

37. Austin F. Hawes, *Second Annual Report of the State Forester on the Progress of Forestry in Vermont* (Montpelier, Vt.: Capital City Press, 1910), 2.

38. Ibid., 2, 23, 24.

39. Louis S. Murphy, P. A. Herbert, and Wade E. DeVries, *Progress Report of the Forest Taxation Inquiry: Digest of Forest Tax Laws in the United States in Effect January 1, 1932* (Washington, D.C.: United States Department of Agriculture, Forest Service, January 1, 1932), 52–54. See *General Laws of Vermont*, 1917, secs. 721–731, as amended by *Laws of Vermont*, 1919, nos. 28 and 19. See also early forestry annual reports.

40. Hawes, *Second Annual Report*, 13, 14; and Merrill, *History of Forestry in Vermont*, 37.

41. Merrill, *History of Forestry in Vermont*, 37, 38.

42. E. S. Brigham, *Eleventh Biennial Report of the Commissioner of Agriculture and the State Forester of the State of Vermont, 1920–22* (St. Albans, Vt.: St. Albans Messenger Co., 1922), 90, 96, 103, 106.

43. Ibid., 106.

44. University of Vermont and State Agricultural College, *Vermont Agricultural Experiment Station Bulletin No. 103: The Maple Sap Flow* (Burlington, Vt.: Free Press Association, December 1903), 49.

45. Albert P. Sy, "History, Manufacture and Analysis of Maple Products," *Journal of the Franklin Institute* (October 1908): 257–59; and University of Vermont and State Agricultural College, *Bulletin No. 103: The Maple Sap Flow*, 52.

46. Sy, "History, Manufacture and Analysis of Maple Products," 257–59; University of Vermont and State Agricultural College, *Bulletin No. 103: The Maple Sap Flow*, 52; and United States Tariff Commission, *Maple Sugar and Maple Sirup: Report of the United States Tariff Commission to the President of the United States* (Washington, D.C., 1930), 21.

47. United States Tariff Commission, *Maple Sugar and Maple Sirup*, 4.

48. University of Vermont and State Agricultural College, *Vermont Agricultural Experiment Station Bulletin No. 285: Economics of the Farm Manufacture of Maple Syrup and Sugar*, by John A. Hitchcock (Burlington, Vt.: Free Press Association, December 1928), 6.

49. Vermont Maple Sugar Makers' Association, *Pure Vermont Maple Sugar, Maple Syrup: Home of the Sugar Maple* (St. Albans, Vt.: Vermont Maple Sugar Makers' Association, December 1912), 20. The association was founded in 1893 to promote quality standards and branding of "Vermont" maple products (28).

50. United States Tariff Commission, *Maple Sugar and Maple Sirup*, 4.

51. William F. Hubbard, *Maple Sugar and Sirup: United States Department of Agriculture Farmers' Bulletin No. 252* (Washington, D.C.: Government Printing Office, 1906), 35.

52. Vermont Maple Sugar Makers' Association, *Pure Vermont Maple Sugar*, 10.

53. Sy, "History, Manufacture and Analysis of Maple Products," 258, 259.

54. Vermont Maple Sugar Makers' Association, *Pure Vermont Maple Sugar*, 10.

55. United States Tariff Commission, *Maple Sugar and Maple Sirup*, 9, 11; Lois Goodwin Greer, "America's Maple Sugar King: George C. Cary," *Vermonter* 34, no. 1 (January 1929): 1–9.

56. Vermont Maple Sugar Makers' Association, *Pure Vermont Maple Sugar*, 23.

57. Greer, "America's Maple Sugar King," 1.

58. Ibid., 4, 5. Cary quotation is from page 4.

59. See Melvin R. Koelling and Randall B. Heiligmann, eds., *North American Maple Sugar Producers Manual* (Columbus: Ohio State University Press, 1996).

60. H. H. Chadwick, *Vermont's Tourist Business: A Study Covering Ten Years* (Burlington, Vt.: Free Press, August 1944), 8.

61. See, for example, Lois Goodwin Greer, "Katharine Ide Gray," *Vermonter* 32 (1927): 195–98, on the founding of the Maple Grove Candies Company and Maple Grove Products of Vermont, both of St. Johnsbury, Vermont, which involved the operation of both mail order and storefront business, a tearoom, and an inn. In addition, Katherine Ide Gray founded a restaurant and shop, Maple Grove Products, on Fifty-seventh Street in New York City, which was managed by her daughter's husband. Greer writes, "Genuine Vermont dishes, real farm products and maple sugar mixtures are served in the 57th Street shop in New York. To make it all a bit more realistic the walls are decorated with scenes from the Vermont hills in maple sugar time, while rustic maple saplings used here and there add a dash of zest and a breath of the country" (197). The Maple Grove businesses were eventually sold to the Cary Maple Sugar Company. See Federal Writers' Project, *Vermont: A Guide to the Green Mountain State* (Boston: Houghton Mifflin, 1937), 141.

62. Gordon G. Whitney, "Sugar Maple: Abundance and Site Relationships in the Pre- and Post-Settlement Forest," in *Sugar Maple Ecology and Health: Proceedings of an International Symposium*, USDA General Technical Report NE-261, eds. S. B. Horsley and R. P. Long (Radnor, Pa.: United States Department of Agriculture, 1999), 14–16.

63. W. W. Ashe, "A National Forest for Vermont," *Vermonter* 36, no. 3 (March 1931): 74.

64. Klyza and Trombulak, *Story of Vermont*, 99, 103, 104; and Ashe, "National Forest for Vermont," 73.

65. John Aubrey Douglass, "The Forest Service, the Depression, and Vermont

Political Culture: Implementing New Deal Conservation and Relief Policy," *Forest and Conservation History* (October 1990): 164.

66. Otto G. Koenig, "Green Mountain National Forest in Vt.," *Vermonter* 44, no. 12 (December 1939): 264.

67. Ibid.

68. Chas R. Cummings, "Plymouth Forestry Camp," *Vermonter* 38, nos. 6–7 (June–July 1933): 139.

69. Koenig, "Green Mountain National Forest in Vt.," 266.

70. Douglass, "Forest Service," 169–72. See also Richard Munson Judd, *The New Deal in Vermont: Its Impact and Aftermath* (New York: Garland, 1979), 82–83.

71. Klyza and Trombulak, *Story of Vermont*, 101; Douglass, "Forest Service," 171.

72. Klyza and Trombulak, *Story of Vermont*, 101; Douglass, "Forest Service," 171; and Harrison, *The View From Vermont*, 123–31.

73. Klyza and Trombulak, *Story of Vermont*, 100.

74. Thomas Birch, *Private Forest-Land Owners of the Northern United States*, Resource Bulletin NE-136 (Washington, D.C.: United States Department of Agriculture, Forest Service, Northeastern Forest Experiment Station, November 1996), 11, 108, 115.

75. Arthur Wallace Peach, *Contemporary Vermont Writers* (Northfield, Vt.: Norwich University Publications, June 1927), 46.

FOUR / WHO OWNS MAINE'S TREES?

1. Julia A. Hunter and Earle G. Shettleworth Jr., *Fly Rod Crosby: The Woman Who Marketed Maine* (Gardiner, Maine: Tilbury House, 2000), 21–22; "Delight for Sportsmen," *New York Times*, 14 May 1895, 7; and "Sporting Scenes Reproduced," *New York Times*, 5 May 1895, 6.

2. Hunter and Shettleworth, *Fly Rod Crosby*, 21–22.

3. Henry David Thoreau, *The Maine Woods* (Boston: Ticknor and Fields, 1864), 70.

4. Fannie Pearson Hardy, "Tales of the Maine Woods: Two Forest and Stream Essays," ed. Pauleena MacDougal, special issue, *Northeast Folklore* 34 (1999).

5. Letters in box 21 (Correspondence and Memorandums Relating to E Aroostook Plantation), Records of the Maine Land Office, Maine State Archives (hereafter cited as E Aroostook Plantation, MLO).

6. See Richard G. Wood, *A History of Lumbering in Maine, 1820–1861*, University of Maine Studies, 2nd series, no. 33 (Orono: University of Maine Press, 1935); David

C. Smith, *A History of Lumbering in Maine, 1861–1960*, University of Maine Studies, 2nd series, no. 93 (Orono: University of Maine Press, 1972); Philip T. Coolidge, *History of the Maine Woods* (Bangor, Maine: Furbish-Roberts Printing Company, 1963); James B. Vickery, Richard W. Judd, and Sheila McDonald, "Maine Agriculture, 1783–1861," in *Maine: The Pine Tree State from Prehistory to the Present*, ed. Richard W. Judd, Edwin A. Churchill, and Joel W. Eastman (Orono: University of Maine Press, 1995); Maine Land Agent, *Annual Report of the Land Agent of the State of Maine, for the Year 1854* (Augusta, Maine: William T. Johnson, Printer to the State, 1855), 8; Richard W. Judd, *Aroostook: A Century of Logging in Northern Maine* (Orono: University of Maine Press, 1989), 73–74; Maine Land Agent, *Annual Report of the Land Agent of the State of Maine for the Year Ending November 30, 1880* (Augusta, Maine: Sprague and Son, Printers to the State, 1881), 3; and Jamie H. Eves, " 'Shrunk to a Comparative Rivulet': Deforestation, Stream Flow, and Rural Milling in 19th-Century Maine," *Technology and Culture* 32, no. 1 (1992): 38–65. Eves estimates that "more than a third of Maine, in the north and east, was unsuitable for agriculture" (48). Also, he figures that by 1880, about half of Maine was deforested, once lumbering, fire, and agriculture are all taken into account (51).

7. Alfred Runte, *National Parks: The American Experience*, 3rd ed. (Lincoln: University of Nebraska Press, 1997), 114–15.

8. Liz Soares, *All for Maine: The Story of Governor Percival P. Baxter* (Mount Desert, Maine: Windswept House, 1995).

9. Percival P. Baxter, *Mount Katahdin State Park: An Address Given by Percival P. Baxter of Portland, President of the Senate, at the Annual Meeting of the Maine Sportsmen's Fish and Game Association* (Augusta, Maine: 1921), 6.

10. Soares, *All for Maine*, 48, 59, 63, 89. See *Maine, New Hampshire and Vermont*, map (Heathrow, Fla.: American Automobile Association, 1997).

11. Smith, *History of Lumbering in Maine, 1861–1960*, 4; and Table 717, "Wood Pulp Production: Total and by States and Processes," in *Statistical Abstracts of the United States, 1930*, 52nd number (Washington, D.C.: GPO, 1930).

12. Judd, *Aroostook*, 72–73, 206, 213–14.

13. Smith, *History of Lumbering in Maine, 1861–1960*, 4, 14, 242, 249; Donald Forrest Dennis, "An Economic Analysis of Harvest Behavior: Integrating Ownership and Forest Characteristics" (PhD diss., Yale University, 1988), 3; and Gerald Ogden, "Forestry for a Nation: The Making of a National Forest Policy under the Weeks and Clarke-McNary Acts, 1900–1924" (PhD diss., University of New Mexico, 1980).

14. Maine Development Commission, *Agricultural Survey Committee, Report of the Agricultural Survey Committee of the Maine Development Commission on Progress in Maine Agriculture, 1850–1920* (Augusta: Maine Development Commission, February 12, 1929), 5, 7.

15. George F. Talbot, "Forest Planting and Municipal Ownership of Forest Lands," in Maine Forest Commissioner, *First Annual Report of the Forest Commissioner of the State of Maine, 1891* (Augusta, Maine: Burleigh and Flint, Printers to the State, 1892), 54.

16. Wood, *History of Lumbering in Maine, 1820–1861*, 196–97.

17. Ibid., 86–87, 196–97.

18. Ibid., 24.

19. Talbot, "Forest Planting and Municipal Ownership of Forest Lands," 52.

20. C. A. Brautlecht, foreword to *A History of Lumbering in Maine, 1820–1861*, University of Maine Studies, 2nd series, no. 33, by Richard G. Wood (Orono: University of Maine Press, 1935).

21. "Memorial in behalf of the Board of Agriculture, to the Legislature of Maine," H. doc. 56, *Legislative Documents*, 1869, 2.

22. "Memorial in behalf of the Board of Agriculture," 1869, 3; and Marsh, *Man and Nature* (see chap. 1, n. 10).

23. "Memorial in behalf of the Board of Agriculture," 1869, 3, 4.

24. Ibid., 21.

25. Smith, *History of Lumbering in Maine, 1861–1960*, 239, 249–55.

26. Edward D. Ives, *George Magoon and the Down East Game War: History, Folklore, and the Law* (Urbana: University of Illinois Press, 1988), 65–69; George F. Godfrey, "The Relation and Importance of Our Forests to Summer Tourists, Sportsmen, Etc.," in Maine Forest Commissioner, *First Annual Report of the Forest Commissioner of the State of Maine, 1891* (Augusta, Maine: Burleigh and Flint, Printers to the State, 1892), 42; and Maine Forest Commissioner, *Seventh Report of the Forest Commissioner of the State of Maine, 1908* (Waterville, Maine: Sentinel, 1908), 28.

27. Maine Land Agent, *Annual Report for 1854*, 7; Wood, *History of Lumbering in Maine, 1820–1861*, 66–67.

28. March O. McCubrey, "The Cultural Construction of Maine Sporting Camps," *Maine History* 34, no. 2 (Fall 1994): 122; Maine Forest Commissioner, *Second Annual Report of the Forest Commissioner, 1894* (Augusta, Maine: Burleigh and Flint, Printers to the State, 1894), 13.

29. Hunter and Shettleworth, *Fly Rod Crosby*, 15.

30. McCubrey, "Cultural Construction of Maine Sporting Camps," 118, 132; Godfrey, "Relation and Importance of Our Forests to Summer Tourists, Sportsmen, Etc.," 43.

31. Fannie Pearson Hardy, "In the Region Around Nicatowis: In Transitu," *Forest and Stream* 35, no. 26 (1890): 510 (reprinted in "Tales of the Maine Woods: Two Forest and Stream Essays," ed. Pauleena MacDougal, special issue, *Northeast Folklore* 34 [1999]: 15).

32. Pauleena MacDougal, introduction to "Tales of the Maine Woods: Two Forest and Stream Essays," ed. Pauleena MacDougal, special issue, *Northeast Folklore* 34 (1999): 7.

33. MacDougal, introduction to "Tales of the Maine Woods," 2.

34. Judd, *Aroostook*, 214; and Fannie Pearson Hardy, "Six Years under Maine Game Laws: Who Owns the Deer? Farmer Speaks," *Forest and Stream* 36, no. 10 (1891): 510 (reprinted in "Tales of the Maine Woods: Two Forest and Stream Essays," ed. Pauleena MacDougal, special issue, *Northeast Folklore* 34 [1999]: 62–63). See also Louis Warren, *The Hunter's Game: Poachers and Conservationists in Twentieth-Century America* (New Haven, Conn.: Yale University Press, 1997), 11–20.

35. *James v. Wood*, 82 Maine Reports 173 (Supreme Judicial Court 1890); *Staples v. Peabody*, 83 Maine Reports 207 (Supreme Judicial Court 1891); and Hardy, "Six Years under Maine Game Laws."

36. Hardy, "Six Years under Maine Game Laws"; and Ives, *George Magoon*, 61–89.

37. Godfrey, "Relation and Importance of Our Forests to Summer Tourists, Sportsmen, Etc.," 44; and Maine Forest Commissioner, *Seventh Report of the Forest Commissioner of the State of Maine, 1908*, 28.

38. Fannie Pearson Hardy, "In Conclusion," *Forest and Stream* 37, no. 3 (1891): 45–46 (reprinted in "Tales of the Maine Woods: Two Forest and Stream Essays," ed. Pauleena MacDougal, special issue, *Northeast Folklore* 34 (1999): 102).

39. Maine Forest Commissioner, *First Annual Report of the Forest Commissioner of the State of Maine, 1891* (Augusta, Maine: Burleigh and Flint, Printers to the State, 1892), 3, 5, 11.

40. Maine Forest Commissioner, *First Annual Report of the Forest Commissioner of the State of Maine, 1891*, 5, 19; Maine Forest Commissioner, *Second Annual Report of the Forest Commissioner of the State of Maine, 1894*, 13; and Michael Williams, *Americans and Their Forests: A Historical Geography* (Cambridge: Cambridge University Press, 1989), 233, 448. All quotations from page 19 of the 1891 report.

41. Judd, *Aroostook*, 211–12.

42. Ibid., 212; Maine Forest Commissioner, *Fifth Report of the Forest Commissioner of the State of Maine, 1904* (Augusta, Maine: Kennebec Journal Print, 1904), 5.

43. Judd, *Aroostook*, 216, 221.

44. Robert Hafford and F. L. Drake to Edgar E. Ring, 17 June 1903, folder 1903; Robert Hafford to Edgar E. Ring, 4 August 1904, folder 1904; and Edwin McGray to Edward E. Ring, 10 April 1908, folder 1904, 1908–1909, all in E Aroostook Plantation, MLO.

45. Olive Cousins to Edgar E. Ring, 4 January 1903, folder 1903, E Aroostook Plantation, MLO.

46. Olive Cousins to Edgar E. Ring, 4 January 1903, folder 1903; Olive Cousins to Edgar E. Ring, 24 January 1903, folder 1903; and Olive Cousins to Edgar E. Ring, 11 January 1905, folder 1904–1907, all in E Aroostook Plantation, MLO.

47. Olive Cousins to Edgar E. Ring, 24 January 1903, folder 1903; Olive Cousins to Edgar E. Ring, 11 January 1905, folder 1904–1907; R. Hafford to Edgar E. Ring, 22 January 1905, folder 1904–1907; R. Hafford to Edgar E. Ring, 9 April 1908, folder 1904–1907; Edwin McGray to Edgar E. Ring, 10 April 1908, folder 1904–1907; and R. Hafford to State Forest Commissioner, 1912, folder 12, all in E Aroostook Plantation, MLO.

48. W. W. Stetson, *History and Government of Maine* (Chicago: Werner School Book Company, 1898), 146.

49. See, for example, Charles Green to Edgar E. Ring, 20 August 1902, box 14 (Correspondence and Memorandums Relating to Coplin Plantation), folder 1901–1902, MLO; and J. S. Williams, Attorney at Law, to Land Owners of Plantation 21, box 78 (Correspondence and Memorandums Relating to Plantation 21, Washington County), folder 1902–1905, MLO. A further complication arose from the fact that a town could also give up its town status and become a plantation. In such a situation, the state would then be required to assume responsibility for the management of the lots that had previously been managed by the town. If the town had chosen to sell its lots rather than manage them for income, a plantation might find itself with no public lots. Record keeping was often spotty, and plantation residents sometimes had difficulty documenting to the state and to new residents that they were justifiably without public land. See, for example, Charles E. Oaks to E. F. Drew, Chairman of the Assessors of Elliottsville Plantation, 6 June 1901, box 22 (Correspondence and Memorandums Relating to Elliottsville Plantation), folder 1900–1901, MLO; F. T. Blackwell to Edgar E. Ring, 22 December 1901,

box 14 (Correspondence and Memorandums Relating to Coplin Plantation), folder 1901–1902, MLO; and E. W. Getchell and Thomas Ladd, Assessors of Barnard Plantation, to Edgar E. Ring, 26 May 1902, box 3 (Correspondence and Memorandums Relating to Barnard Plantation), folder 1902, MLO.

50. Maine Forest Commissioner, *Annual Report of the Land Agent of the State of Maine, for the year ending November 30, 1892* (Augusta, Maine: Burleigh and Flint, Printers to the State, 1893), 4; Maine State Archives, *Counties, Cities, Towns and Plantations of Maine* (Augusta: Maine State Archives, 1940), 65; and Stanley Bearce Attwood, *The Length and Breadth of Maine* (Orono: University of Maine at Orono Press, 1977), 31.

51. See, for example, Chas. E. Ball, Superintendent of Schools, to Edgar E. Ring, 9 June 1912, box 7 (Correspondence and Memorandums Relating to Caratunk Plantation), folder 1911–1912, MLO; Edgar E. Ring to Bert L. Spaulding, Chairman of Assessors, Caratunk Plantation, 8 September 1915, box 7 (Correspondence and Memorandums Relating to Caratunk Plantation), folder 1915, MLO; Noah Bernbay, Assessor of Caswell, to Edgar E. Ring, 9 December 1903, box 10 (Correspondence and Memorandums Relating to Caswell Plantation), folder 1902–1903, MLO; and Lewis S. Crosby to Frank E. Mace, 31 October 1911, box 78 (Correspondence and Memorandums Relating to Plantation 21, Washington County), folder 1911, MLO.

52. See, for example, Henry H. Jewell to Edgar E. Ring, 24 May 1908; Henry H. Jewell to Edgar E. Ring, 30 May 1908; and Henry H. Jewell to Edgar E. Ring, 12 October 1908, all in box 10 (Correspondence and Memorandums Relating to Caswell Plantation), folder 1908, MLO.

53. Lewis Crosby to Frank E. Mace, 25 October 1911, box 78 (Correspondence and Memorandums Relating to Plantation 21, Washington County), folder 1911, MLO.

54. Frank E. Mace to Assessors of Plantation 21, 6 October 1911; and Frank E. Mace to Irving [Irwin] R. Sprague, 10 October 1911, both in box 78 (Correspondence and Memorandums Relating to Plantation 21, Washington County), folder 1911, MLO.

55. Lewis Crosby to Frank E. Mace, 31 October 1911, box 78 (Correspondence and Memorandums Relating to Plantation 21, Washington County), folder 1911, MLO.

56. Noah Berube to Frank E. Mace, 26 October 1915, folder 1915; Frank E. Mace to Noah J. Berube, 27 October 1915, folder 1915; Eugia Berube to State Land Agent,

16 December 1915, folder 1915; and Eugia Berube to Frank E. Mace, 8 January 1916, folder 1916, all in box 10 (Correspondence and Memorandums Relating to Caswell Plantation), MLO.

57. Noah Bernbay, Assessor of Caswell, to Edgar E. Ring, 9 December 1903, box 10 (Correspondence and Memorandums Relating to Caswell Plantation), folder 1902–1903, MLO.

58. Robert Hafford to E. E. Ring, 4 September 1904; and Robert Hafford to E. E. Ring, 9 April 1908, both in folder 1904, 1908–1909, E Aroostook Plantation, MLO.

59. Olive Cousins to Edgar Ring, 4 January 1903, folder 1903; Olive Cousins to Edgar Ring, 24 January 1904, folder 1903; Olive Cousins to Edgar Ring, 11 January 1905, folder 1904–1907; Robert Hafford to E. E. Ring, 22 January 1905, folder 1904–1907; and Edwin McGray to Edgar Ring, 10 April 1908, folder 1904, 1908–1909, all in E Aroostook Plantation, MLO.

60. F. L. Harvey, "Preservation of Our Forests," in Maine Forest Commissioner, *First Annual Report of the Forest Commissioner of the State of Maine, 1891*, 33; Francis Wiggin, "The Preservation of Maine Forests and Lake and Park Reservations: An Address," address delivered before the State Board of Trade at Rockland, Maine, October 15th, 1901 (Portland, Maine: Marks Printing House, 1901–2), 15; Baxter, *Mount Katahdin State Park*, 5; and "Do We Want a Maine National Forest?" *Lewiston Journal*, 27 September 1935 (clipping, Austin Cary Papers, box 1663, folder "Maine Forestry By Austin Cary," Special Collections, University of Maine, Orono). For a comparison of forest protection efforts in Maine and New Hampshire and their relationship to land ownership patterns, see Richard W. Judd, *Common Lands, Common People: The Origins of Conservation in Northern New England* (Cambridge, Mass.: Harvard University Press, 1997), 99–120.

61. See Lloyd Irland, "Maine Forests: A Century of Change, 1900–2000, and Elements of Policy Change for a New Century," *Maine Policy Review* (Winter 2000), 66–77; Lloyd Irland, "U.S. Forest Ownership: Historic and Global Perspective," *Maine Policy Review* (Winter 2005), 16–22; *2009 Annual Report for Public Reserved, Non-Reserved, and Submerged Lands to the Joint Standing Committee on Agriculture, Conservation, and Forestry* ([Augusta, Maine]: Maine Department of Conservation Bureau of Parks and Lands, 1 March 2010); and *Maine State Forest Assessment and Strategies Executive Summary* (Augusta, Maine: Department of Conservation, Maine Forest Service, Forest Policy and Management Division, 18 June 2010).

1. Michael J. Feeney, "Bear Breakfasts on Caged Rabbit," *Herald News* (Passaic County, N.J.), 9 July 2009.
2. "Maybe Corzine Will Pay Attention Now That Black Bears Are Running Around Trenton," *State News Service*, 9 September 2009.
3. John McPhee, *Table of Contents* (Farrar, Straus and Giroux, 1986), 13.
4. Robert Hanley, "Young Bear, Picked On, Heads for Paramus Mall," *New York Times*, 30 May 1992; McPhee, *Table of Contents*, 16; and New Jersey Department of Environmental Protection, Division of Fish and Wildlife Service, "Comprehensive Black Bear Management Policy," http://www.state.nj.us/dep/fgw/bearpolicy10.htm.
5. Tiffani N. Garlic, "Furry Visitor Greeted with Nary a Roar; in Manville," *Star Ledger*, 16 September 2009.
6. Cate McQuaid, "The Hush of History: Not All at Quabbin Is a Watery Grave; Relics of People and Towns Remain," *Boston Globe*, 26 January 2003.
7. Thomas Connuel, *Quabbin: The Accidental Wilderness*, rev. ed. (Amherst: University of Massachusetts Press, 1990).
8. Michael Tougias, *Quabbin: A History and Explorers Guide* (Yarmouth Port, Mass.: On Cape Publications, 2002), viii, xv, 4.
9. See National Research Council, *Watershed Management for Potable Water Supply: Assessing the New York City Strategy* (Washington, D.C.: National Academy Press, 2000); and U.S. Environmental Protection Agency, *Protecting Sources of Drinking Water: Selected Case Studies in Watershed Management*, Office of Water EPA publication 816-R-98–019 (April 1999).
10. Eddie Nickens, "A Watershed Paradox: As New York City Struggles to Protect Water Quality and Upstate Forest Lands, the Choices Are Clear: Everybody Wins or Everybody Loses," *American Forests* (Winter 1998): 21–24; Andrew C. Revkin, "New York Begins Spending to Save City's Reservoirs," *New York Times*, 22 January 1997; and "A Watershed Agreement," *New York Times*, 11 September 1996.
11. Nickens, "Watershed Paradox," 22; and Revkin, "New York Begins Spending."
12. Nickens, "Watershed Paradox," 22.
13. Alf Evers, *The Catskills: From Wilderness to Woodstock* (Garden City, N.Y.: Doubleday & Company, 1972), 43–44.

14. David J. Nowak and Eric J. Greenfield, "Urban and Community Forests of the Mid-Atlantic Region: New Jersey, New York, Pennsylvania," United States Department of Agriculture, Forest Service, Northern Research Station General Technical Report NRS-47 (Newtown Square, Pa.: U.S. Forest Service, 2009) (also available online at http://www.nrs.fs.fed.us/pubs/9740), 19.

15. David J. Nowak and Eric J. Greenfield, "Urban and Community Forests of New England: Connecticut, Maine, Massachusetts, New Hampshire, Rhode Island, Vermont," United States Department of Agriculture, Forest Service, Northern Research Station General Technical Report NRS-38 (Newtown Square, Pa.: U.S. Forest Service, 2009) (also available online at http://www.nrs.fs.fed.us/pubs/9199), 27.

16. David R. Foster, David Kittredge, Brian Donahue, Glenn Motzkin, David Orwig, Aaron Ellison, Brian Hall, Betsy Colburn, and Anthony D'Amato, *Wildlands and Woodlands: A Vision for the Forests of New England* (Petersham, Mass.: Harvard Forest, Harvard University, 2005) (also online at http://www. wildlandsandwoodlands.org); Brian Donahue, David Foster, Brian Hall, Bill Labish, Kathy Fallon Lambert, Jim Levitt, Keith Ross, and Loring Shwarz, *Wildlands and Woodlands: Gaining Ground in 2008* (Petersham, Mass.: Harvard Forest, Harvard University, 2008) (also available online at http://www.wildlandsandwoodlands.org); and David R. Foster and William G. Labich, "A Wildland and Woodland Vision for the New England Landscape: Local Conservation, Biodiversity and the Global Environment," in *Saving Biological Diversity: Balancing Protection of Endangered Species and Ecosystems*, ed. Robert A. Askins, Glenn D. Dreyer, Gerald R. Visigilio, and Diana M. Whitelaw (New York: Springer, 2008), 155–75.

17. Foster et al., *Wildlands and Woodlands: A Vision for the Forests of New England*, 4.

18. Robert Sullivan, "The Working Forest," *New York Times*, 19 April 2009; and Foster and Labich, "Wildland and Woodland Vision."

19. Foster et al., *Wildlands and Woodlands: A Vision for the Forests of New England*, 14–16.

20. Ernest Morrison, *J. Horace McFarland: A Thorn for Beauty* (Harrisburg: Pennsylvania Historical and Museum Commission, 1995), 287–95.

21. Douglas Martin, "Wild (and Unleashed) Coyote Is Captured in Central Park," *New York Times*, 2 April 1999; Douglas Martin, "Central Park Coyote Will Live in Queens," *New York Times*, 13 April 1999; "Neighborhood News: Coyote Gets New Home," *The Daily News* (New York), 15 April 1999; Corey Kilgannon,

"Coyote, a Wily Survivor, Is Alpha at His Zoo Home," *New York Times*, 19 March 2000.

22. http://www.queenszoo.com/animals-and-exhibits/exhibits/great-plains.aspx (accessed 4 December 2011).

23. Christpher Ketcham, "A New Trickster in Town," *New York Times*, 3 October 2004; James Barron, "Hal Coyote, 1, Known for Romp in Central Park, Is Dead," *New York Times*, 1 April 2006.

24. For an entertaining discussion of the ubiquity of coyotes in the densely settled modern American landscape, see Stephen DeStefano, *Coyote at the Kitchen Door: Living with Wildlife in Suburbia* (Cambridge, Mass.: Harvard University Press, 2010). See also http://www.nycgovparks.org/greening/wildlife (accessed 30 May 2012).

25. Nicole Lyn Pesce, "Where NY's Wild Things Are: The City Is Getting More Beastly Every Day," *Daily News* (New York), 11 October 2009; John Lauinger, "Coyote's Mad Dash to Freedom," *Daily News* (New York), 25 March 2010; James Barron, "After Night on the Town, a Furry Fugitive in Manhattan Is Captured," *New York Times*, 26 March 2010.

Bibliographic Essay

Writing *Nature Next Door* has led me through diverse primary source material and scholarship from many disciplines, and as my students well know, I can never resist suggesting more reading. While the endnotes give details of my specific use of sources, I offer this brief bibliographic essay as a guide to the collections and materials that most influenced my thinking for this book.

This project found its genesis almost two decades ago in concurrent readings of William Cronon's *Nature's Metropolis: Chicago and the Great West* (New York: W. W. Norton and Co., 1991) and Bill McKibben's *Hope, Human and Wild: True Stories of Living Lightly on the Earth* (Saint Paul, Minn.: Hungry Mind Press, 1995). Both books celebrate nature and the city, forcefully demonstrating the interconnectedness of the two types of landscape, and both suggest an argument that protecting natural systems outside of the city is intimately tied to policies and decisions within urban places. McKibben, in both *Hope* and the more recent *Eaarth* [*sic*]: *Making a Life on a Tough New Planet* (New York: Henry Holt and Co., 2010), steps right to the edge of arguing for dense human settlement as a crucial component of responsible environmental policy, but he ultimately retreats to a pastoral vision that seems to wish cities away. Cronon does no such thing, but his narrative of a booming city eating its hinterland seemed to me both absolutely right for Chicago's time and place and not the necessary trajectory for the coinciding urban and hinterland transformations his analysis reveals. It was possible that in the twentieth-century northeastern United States, the story had a different arc.

Elizabeth Blackmar and Roy Rosenzweig's *The Park and the People: A History of Central Park* (Ithaca, NY: Cornell University Press, 1992) and Kenneth T. Jackson's *Crabgrass Frontier: The Suburbanization of the United States* (New York: Oxford University Press, 1985) got me thinking about the roles of planners and state, federal, and municipal politics in the shaping of both built and seemingly more organic environments of cities and their regions. After moving to New York to work with Blackmar and Jackson at Columbia, I began to rummage in local archives and the growing literature of northeastern environmental history to see how the lives of forests in that corner of the United States differed from stories elsewhere.

In seeking out the ecological, political, and intellectual roots of the dramatic twentieth-century reforestation in the northeastern United States, numerous archival collections were invaluable. The Forest History Society in Durham, North Carolina, is rich in resources for any scholar studying forests, and their collections were key. Likewise, I have drawn heavily on the resources of the Historical Society of Pennsylvania (especially the Herbert Welsh Collection, abbreviated HWC in the notes), the Library Company of Philadelphia, the Pennsylvania State Archives (especially the Mira Dock Collection, abbreviated MDC in the notes), the Pennsylvania Department of Environmental Resources Rachel Carson Collection, the Lake Sunapee Historical Society in New Hampshire, the University of New Hampshire Milne Special Collections and Archives, the New Hampshire State Archives, the Vermont State Archives, the Vermont Historical Society, the Wilbur Collection of the University of Vermont's Bailey/Howe Library, the Maine State Archives (especially the Maine Land Office Records, abbreviated MLO in the notes), and the University of Maine Special Collections.

Anyone interested in the modern history of forests in the United States must certainly begin with Sargent's early survey, Charles S. Sargent, *Report on the Forests of North America (exclusive of Mexico), Tenth Census of the United States, 1880* (Washington, D.C.: Government Printing Office, 1884), along with the wealth of conflicting, confusing, and fun material published by the early foresters of the states, much of which is collected at the Forest History Society, as well as in state archives. Early reports from the U.S. Forest Service are also a treasure trove, as are the many timber and forest industry publications.

In the last two decades, forest historians have made sense of many of the transformations of American forests and forestry for us. Among the best and most comprehensive works are Thomas R. Cox, Robert S. Maxwell, Phillip Drennon Thomas, and Joseph P. Malone, *This Well-Wooded Land: Americans and Their Forests from Colo-*

nial Times to Present (Lincoln: University of Nebraska Press, 1985); Thomas R. Cox, *The Lumberman's Frontier: Three Centuries of Land Use, Society, and Change in America's Forests* (Corvallis: Oregon State University Press, 2010); Char Miller, ed., *American Forests: Nature, Culture, and Politics* (Lawrence: University Press of Kansas, 1997); Gordon Graham Whitney, *From Coastal Wilderness to Fruited Plain: A History of Environmental Change in Temperate North America, 1500 to the Present* (New York: Cambridge University Press, 1994); and Michael Williams, *Americans and their Forests: A Historical Geography* (New York: Cambridge University Press, 1989). While masterly, and necessary launching points for anyone studying American forests, their broad chronological sweep tends to leave the northeastern woods early in the narrative, and by the twentieth century, their stories have more or less taken us to the wooded West.

Another crucial group of books focuses primarily on national policies, and therefore most often on land and trees owned by the federal government rather than the nation's forests as a whole. Of these, Samuel T. Dana and Sally Fairfax's *Forest and Range Policy: Its Development in the United States*, 2nd. ed. (New York: McGraw-Hill, 1980); Paul W. Hirt's *A Conspiracy of Optimism: Management of the National Forests Since World War Two* (Lincoln: University of Nebraska Press, 1994); Douglas W. MacCleery's *American Forests: A History of Resilience and Recovery*, revised ed. (Durham, N.C.: United States Department of Agriculture, Forest Service, with the Forest History Society, 1992; repr. 1993); *The Origins of the National Forests*, edited by Harold K. Steen (Durham, N.C.: Forest History Society, 1992); and Samuel P. Hays, *The American People and the National Forests: The First Century of the U.S. Forest Service* (Pittsburgh, Penn.: University of Pittsburgh Press, 2009) offer crucial context for developments at the local and state level. William G. Robbins, in *American Forestry: A History of National, State, and Private Cooperation* (Lincoln: University of Nebraska Press, 1985) points in those directions, while ultimately remaining national in focus. Hays, in *Wars in the Woods: The Rise of Ecological Forestry in America* (Pittsburgh, Penn.: University of Pittsburgh Press, 2007) not only covers the East Coast in his idiosyncratic take on recent forest policy history, but also offers a chapter on Pennsylvania in particular. Sara M. Gregg, in *Managing the Mountains: Land Use Planning, the New Deal, and the Creation of a Federal Landscape in Appalachia* (New Haven, Conn.: Yale University Press, 2010), stands out in taking the eastern United States as the explicit focus of her work, and she does a beautiful job of weaving federal, state, and local histories together. Her case studies of twentieth-century land-use history in Virginia and Vermont offer a model for understanding the impact of federal policies on northeastern lands.

In recent years, environmental historians have been putting culture, politics, and the history of science squarely at the center of their stories. Though about the West, Nancy Langston's *Forest Dreams, Forest Nightmares: The Paradox of Old Growth in the Inland West* (Seattle: University of Washington Press, 1995) is important for demonstrating the ways in which what people believed they were doing for forests did not always match their results. Louis Warren, in *The Hunter's Game: Poachers and Conservationists in Twentieth-Century America* (New Haven, Conn.: Yale University Press, 1997), and Karl Jacoby, in *Crimes Against Nature: Squatters, Poachers, Thieves, and the Hidden History of American Conservation* (Berkeley: University of California Press, 2001), bring class and cultural history to their histories of forested lands. Richard W. Judd, *Common Lands, Common People: The Origins of Conservation in Northern New England* (Cambridge, Mass.: Harvard University Press, 1997) highlights the active role that farmers played in shaping the possibilities for forest preservation and cultivation in the Northeast. Theodore Steinberg's *Nature Incorporated: Industrialization and the Waters of New England* (Amherst: University of Massachusetts Press, 1991) is the best legal environmental history of the region.

For northeastern forests in particular, Harold Fisher Wilson's *The Hill Country of Northern New England: Its Social and Economic History, 1790–1930* (New York: Columbia University Press, 1936) remains an important contextual work. William Cronon, *Changes in the Land: Indians, Colonists, and the Ecology of New England* (New York: Hill and Wang, 1983) continues to be the best introduction to the early environmental history of the region. David R. Conrad, *The Land We Cared For: A History of the Forest Service's Eastern Region* (Milwaukee, Wisc.: United States Department of Agriculture, Forest Service Region 9, 1997); John T. Cumbler, *Reasonable Use: The People, The Environment, and the State, New England 1790–1930* (Oxford: Oxford University Press, 2001); David Dobbs and Richard Ober, *The Northern Forest* (White River Junction, Vt.: Chelsea Green Publishing Co., 1995); and Christopher McGrory Klyza and Stephen C. Trombulak, eds., *The Future of the Northern Forest* (Hanover, N.H.: University Press of New England, 1994) bring the focus into the twentieth century. David R. Foster and John D. Aber, eds., *Forests in Time: The Environmental Consequences of 1,000 Years of Change in New England* (New Haven, Conn.: Yale University Press, 2004) is both broad and deep, and is a critical resource for anyone who wants to understand the specifics of New England forest history on the grandest scale. Also crucial, if sometimes sprawling, are Lloyd C. Irland, *The Northeast's Changing Forest* (Petersham, Mass.: distributed by Harvard University Press for Harvard Forest, 1999) and *Wildlands and Woodlots: The Story of New England's Forests* (Hanover, N.H.: University Press of New England, 1982).

David R. Foster and John F. O'Keefe's *New England Forests Through Time: Insights from the Harvard Forest Dioramas* (Petersham, Mass.: Harvard Forest, 2000) offers a unique and delightful approach to the region's forest history, reading not just the landscape but also the dioramas of the Harvard Forest created in the 1930s, which are on display at the Harvard Forest's Fischer Museum.

In addition to Judd, a number of other scholars have placed rural people in their rightfully prominent place in northeastern environmental history, some looking region-wide, and others focusing on particular states. Hal S. Barron, *Mixed Harvest: The Second Transformation in the Rural North, 1970–1930* (Chapel Hill: University of North Carolina Press, 1997) and *Those Who Stayed Behind: Rural Society in Nineteenth-Century New England* (Cambridge: Cambridge University Press, 1984) take a broad view. Blake Harrison, *The View From Vermont: Tourism and the Making of an American Rural Landscape* (Burlington: University of Vermont Press, 2006); Christopher McGrory Klyza and Stephen C. Trombulak, *The Story of Vermont: A Natural and Cultural History* (Hanover, N.H.: University Press of New England / Middlebury College Press, 1999); and Harold A. Meeks, *Time and Change in Vermont: A Human Geography* (Chester, Conn.: The Globe Pequot Press, 1986) focus more specifically on Vermont. Richard W. Judd, *Aroostook: A Century of Logging in Northern Maine* (Orono: University of Maine Press, 1989); Richard W. Judd, Edwin A. Churchill, and Joel W. Eastman, *Maine: The Pine Tree State from Prehistory to the Present* (Orono: University of Maine Press, 1995); and Alan Taylor, *Liberty Men and Great Proprietors: The Revolutionary Settlement on the Maine Frontier, 1760–1820* (Chapel Hill: University of North Carolina Press, 1990) all focus on Maine. David Stradling's *Making Mountains: New York City and the Catskills* (Seattle: University of Washington Press, 2007), highlights the intertwined environmental histories of New York City and its hinterlands. Charles H. W. Foster, in *Stepping Back to Look Forward: A History of the Massachusetts Forest* (Cambridge, Mass.: Harvard University Press, 1998), provides both a thoughtful history of forests in Massachusetts and also a useful guide for investigating the forest history of the other states in the region. Brian Donahue's *The Great Meadow: Farmers and the Land in Colonial Concord* (New Haven, Conn.: Yale University Press, 2004) and *Reclaiming the Commons: Community Farms and Forests in a New England Town* (New Haven, Conn.: Yale University Press, 1999) are models as well, telling the Massachusetts story in a more lyrical and local way.

Blake Harrison's *The View from Vermont* highlights the importance of tourism in the shaping of the region's woods, as do Dona Brown's *Inventing New England: Regional Tourism in the Nineteenth Century* (Washington, D.C.: Smithsonian Institution Press, 1995) and *A Tourist's New England: Travel Fiction, 1820–1920* (Hanover, N.H.: Hardscrabble Books, 1999). Kimberly A. Jarvis, *Franconia Notch and the Women Who Saved It* (Durham: University of New Hampshire Press, 2007) explores not only the importance of tourism and outdoor recreation in northeastern forest history, but also the central role that women had in conservation politics both in New Hampshire and elsewhere.

A number of the characters who appear in *Nature Next Door*, both women and men, are the subjects of entertaining and informative biographies. Julia A. Hunter and Earle G. Shettleworth Jr., *Fly Rod Crosby: The Woman Who Marketed Maine* (Gardiner, Maine: Tilbury House, 2000); Char Miller, *Gifford Pinchot and the Making of Modern Environmentalism* (Washington, D.C.: Island Press, 2001); and Ernest Morrison, *J. Horace MacFarland: A Thorn for Beauty* (Harrisburg: Pennsylvania Historical and Museum Commission, 1995) are all worth a read, as is Pauleena MacDougal's introductory essay to her edited volume "Tales of the Maine Woods: Two Forest and Stream Essays, by Fannie Pearson Hardy" [*Northeast Folklore* (Orono, Maine) 34 (1999)]. David R. Foster's *Thoreau's Country: Journey Through a Transformed Landscape* (Cambridge, Mass.: Harvard University Press, 1999) is quirky and fun, offering snapshots of New England's environmental history through short essays (primarily descriptive, but sometimes analytical) followed by mosaics of quotations from Henry David Thoreau.

Along with Cronon's *Nature's Metropolis*, other important works of urban environmental history informed and shaped this book, including Sarah S. Elkind, *Bay Cities and Water Politics: The Battle for Resources in Boston and Oakland* (Lawrence: University Press of Kansas, 1998); Ari Kelman, *A River and Its City: The Nature of Landscape in New Orleans* (Berkeley: University of California Press, 2003); Matthew Klingle, *Emerald City: An Environmental History of Seattle* (New Haven, Conn.: Yale University Press, 2007); Martin Melosi, *The Sanitary City: Urban Infrastructure in America from Colonial Times to Present* (Baltimore: Johns Hopkins University Press, 2000); Anne Whiston Spirn, *The Granite Garden: Urban Nature and Human Design* (New York: Basic Books, 1984); Joel Tarr, *The Search for the Ultimate Sink: Urban Pollution in Historical Perspective* (Akron, Ohio: University of Akron Press, 1996) and Joel Tarr, ed., *Devastation and Renewal: An Environmental History of Pittsburgh and Its Region* (Pittsburgh: University of Pittsburgh Press, 2005).

McKibben's *Hope, Human and Wild* and MacCleery's *American Forests* are among a growing body of cautiously optimistic environmental writing. John Elder, *Reading the Mountains of Home* (Cambridge, Mass.: Harvard University Press, 1998); Christopher McGrory Klyza, ed., *Wilderness Comes Home: Rewilding the Northeast* (Hanover, N.H.: University Press of New England, 2001); and Tom Wessels, *Reading the Forested*

Landscape: A Natural History of New England (Woodstock, Vt.: The Countryman Press, 1997) are all cheerful reads. Gregg Easterbrook, *A Moment on the Earth: The Coming Age of Environmental Optimism* (New York: Penguin Books, 1995) is also, as the title suggests, optimistic, but it ultimately goes too far, arguing that stories of recovery and resilience demonstrate that nature will always bounce back. That could be true, but as McKibben makes clear in *Eaarth* (without pursuing all of the implications), there might not be a place for people in those new ecologies. Likewise, Charles E. Little, in *The Dying of the Trees: The Pandemic in America's Forests* (New York: Penguin Books, 1997) offers a useful dose of despair.

In some ways, Easterbrook echoes Hugh M. Raup's "The View from John Sanderson's Farm: A Perspective for the Use of the Land" [*Forest History* 10, no. 1 (April 1966): 2–11], in which Raup argues that evidence at the Harvard Forest demonstrates that aggressive landscape management is both misguided and unnecessary. Brian Donahue, in "Another Look from Sanderson's Farm: A Perspective on New England Environmental History and Conservation" [*Environmental History* 12, no. 1 (January 2007): 9–34], critiques that perspective and brings a necessary caution to trusting nature to choose its own course.

Additional practical optimism is offered by David R. Foster, David Kittredge, Brian Donahue, Glenn Motzkin, David Orwig, Aaron Ellison, Brian Hall, Betsy Colburn, and Anthony D'Amato in *Wildlands and Woodlands: A Vision for the Forests of New England* (Petersham, Mass.: Harvard Forest, 2005) and Brian Donahue, David R. Foster, Brian Hall, Bill Labish, Kathy Fallon Lambert, Jim Levitt, Keith Ross, and Loring Shwarz in *Wildlands and Woodlands: Gaining Ground in 2008* (Petersham, Mass.: Harvard Forest, 2008). Their collaborative vision for planning and managing multiplicities of landscapes to nurture both human and non-human nature will take hard work, and harder work still if it is to be realized on not just a regional but a global scale. Their work is about the future, but is grounded in understanding the past.

Index

Entries in boldface type refer to illustrations.

U.S. Environmental Protection Agency, 25, 151
U.S. Forest Service, 13–14, 23, 30, 75, 108, 152

Vermont, 28, 81–82, 148; differences between, and New Hampshire, 80, 81, 82, 91, 96, 100, 107; farms in: *see* Vermont farms; forest cover in, 5, 87, **89**, 96, 178n10; Green Mountain National Forest in, 53, 110, **159**; and railroads, 88–90, 91–92, 93, 179n16; romantic images of, 113–14; state forests in, 96, 99, 111; tax policies in, 97–99; tourism in, 82, 85–87, 92–95, 107, 130–32, 177n3; varieties of trees in, 96, 99, 100, 107 (*see also* sugar maple trees)
Vermont Board of Agriculture, 82, 92
Vermont Bureau of Publicity, 82, 85
Vermonter magazine, 108
Vermont farms, 96, 111; continued viability of, 82, 92; and dairying, 90, 91–92, 93, 104; and maple products, 102–6; and tourism, 82, 85–87, 92–95, 107, 177n3; tree planting on, 97–100
Vermont Forest Reservation Commission, 108
Vermont Forestry Commission, 96, 99. *See also* Hawes, Austin
Vermont Maple Sugar Makers' Association, 104, 182n54
viewsheds, 53, 57

Waltham, Mass., 59
Wasserscheide, 57
water pollution, 24–25, 31

water power, 56–57, 59, 66
watersheds, 57–58; beliefs about, 25, 30–31, 47; campaigns for protection of, 33, 42–44, 48, 53, 73–74
water supply. *See* water power; drinking water supplies
Weeks Act (1911), 53, 57, 68, 77, 108; land purchases under, 53, 77–78, 108
Welsh, Herbert, 3, 33, 46, 48, 146; on connection between city and hinterland, 5–7, 146, 155; long-distance walks by, 3–4, 5, 15, 146; national influence of, 48, 65; and New Hampshire forests, 48, 50, 57, 65, 66, 68–70, 75, 76
Wetzel's Swamp, 43, 44, 155
Wheelock, W. B., 84
White, Alan, 151
White Mountain National Forest, 53, 56, 77, 78, 110; impetus for creation of, 107
White Mountains, 59, 73–74. *See also* White Mountain National Forest
"wildlands," 121, 152
Wildlands and Woodlands proposal, 152–54
Wilgus, William J., 90
Will, Thomas, 46
Winans family (Vermont), 92–93
wood pulp, 96, 121, 123
World War II, 106
Wren, Christopher, 15, 146, 155

Yuhas, Darlene, 145

WEYERHAEUSER ENVIRONMENTAL BOOKS

The Promise of Wilderness: American Environmental Politics since 1964
by James Morton Turner
Pumpkin: The History of an American Icon
by Cindy Ott
Nature Next Door: Cities and Trees in the American Northeast
by Ellen Stroud
Car Country: An Environmental History
by Christopher W. Wells

WEYERHAEUSER ENVIRONMENTAL CLASSICS

The Great Columbia Plain: A Historical Geography, 1805–1910
by D. W. Meinig
Mountain Gloom and Mountain Glory: The Development of the Aesthetics of the Infinite
by Marjorie Hope Nicolson
Tutira: The Story of a New Zealand Sheep Station
by Herbert Guthrie-Smith
A Symbol of Wilderness: Echo Park and the American Conservation Movement
by Mark Harvey
Man and Nature: Or, Physical Geography as Modified by Human Action
by George Perkins Marsh; edited and annotated by David Lowenthal
Conservation in the Progressive Era: Classic Texts
edited by David Stradling
DDT, Silent Spring, and the Rise of Environmentalism: Classic Texts
edited by Thomas R. Dunlap
The Environmental Moment, 1968–1972
by David Stradling

CYCLE OF FIRE
BY STEPHEN J. PYNE

Fire: A Brief History
World Fire: The Culture of Fire on Earth
Vestal Fire: An Environmental History, Told through Fire, of Europe
    and Europe's Encounter with the World
Fire in America: A Cultural History of Wildland and Rural Fire
Burning Bush: A Fire History of Australia
The Ice: A Journey to Antarctica